The Essence of
Financial
Management

The Essence of Management Series

Published titles

The Essence of Total Quality Management
The Essence of Strategic Management
The Essence of International Money
The Essence of Management Accounting
The Essence of Financial Accounting
The Essence of Marketing Research
The Essence of Information Systems
The Essence of Personal Microcomputing
The Essence of Successful Staff Selection
The Essence of Effective Communication
The Essence of Statistics for Business
The Essence of Business Taxation
The Essence of the Economy
The Essence of Mathematics for Business
The Essence of Organizational Behaviour
The Essence of Small Business
The Essence of Business Economics
The Essence of Operations Management
The Essence of Services Marketing
The Essence of International Business
The Essence of Marketing

Forthcoming titles

The Essence of Public Relations
The Essence of Financial Management
The Essence of Business Law
The Essence of International Marketing
The Essence of Women in Management
The Essence of Mergers and Acquisitions
The Essence of Industrial Relations and Personnel Management
The Essence of Influencing Skills
The Essence of Services Management
The Essence of Industrial Marketing
The Essence of Venture Capital and New Ventures

The Essence of Financial Management

D. R. Myddelton

Prentice Hall

New York   London   Toronto   Sydney   Tokyo   Singapore

First published 1995 by
Prentice Hall International (UK) Limited
Campus 400, Maylands Avenue
Hemel Hempstead
Hertfordshire, HP2 7EZ
A division of
Simon & Schuster International Group

Typeset in 10/12pt Palatino
by Keyset Composition, Colchester, Essex

Printed and bound in Great Britain by
Hartnolls Limited, Bodmin, Cornwall

Library of Congress Cataloging-in-Publication Data
Myddelton, David R.
  The essence of financial management /
  David Myddelton.
    p. cm. — (The essence of management series)
  Includes bibliographical references and index.
  ISBN 0-13-284787-6 (pbk.)
  1. Business enterprises—Finance.
  2. Corporations—Finance.
  I. Title. II. Series.
  HG4026.M93 1995
  658.15—dc20   94-35311
                                           CIP

British Library Cataloguing in Publication Data

A catalogue record for this book is available from the
British Library

ISBN 0-13-284787-6 (pbk)

1 2 3 4 5 99 98 97 96 95

Contents

Preface

Financial management is largely about *matching*:

- the maturities of liabilities with the lives of assets;
- the currencies of borrowings with those of earnings; and
- the required rate of return on investments with their risk.

So, as the figure below shows, this book 'matches' four asset chapters (3–6) with four finance ones (7–10). The other three chapters cover both assets and finance: the introduction (Chapter 1), among other topics, outlines the structure of balance sheets; interest rates (Chapter 2) affect not merely the cost of finance, but also the valuation of assets; and in Chapter 11, while mergers combine assets of different firms, reconstructions mainly reallocate interests between creditors and shareholders.

1. Introduction
2. Interest rates

Assets	*Finance*
3. Cash	7. Borrowing
4. Working capital	8. Ordinary shares
Capital project appraisal:	9. Valuing equity
5. Basic	10. Corporate finance
6. Refinements	

11. Mergers and reconstructions

This book probably does contain rather more on assets (and therefore rather less on finance) than most text-books on financial management. There may not be much financial theory relating to working capital, but in many firms current assets represent the bulk of total assets. Managing them properly is thus important. It is critical, for instance, for marketing managers to appreciate the key variables in extending credit to customers, and for production managers to understand the total costs of holding stock. It is no coincidence that management consultants often concentrate first on the management of working capital. They recognize that many firms are weak in this area – not so much because it is difficult, but because it requires continual vigilance.

Capital project appraisal is familiar territory in text-books. This book explains discounted cash flow methods by referring first to the Net Terminal Value method, before moving on to Net Present Value. The reason for this approach is the more explicit discussion of what the interest rate (or discount rate) actually means – it is an 'opportunity cost', representing what else the investing firm could have done with the money. It is more important to understand what the interest rate means than to be the world's leading expert on calculating it to three places of decimals. In general, people – not just students – tend to be absurdly credulous in the accuracy of the 'information' they sometimes assume a company will have available.

The chapter on capital project appraisal refinements contains a detailed analysis of the impact of inflation, and its interaction with tax writing-down allowances and with investment in working capital. The author is now enough of a veteran to have witnessed many Chancellors of the Exchequer over the decades state or hint that we need not worry about inflation in future. At the time of writing UK markets seem to be expecting inflation over the next fifteen years to average nearly 5 per cent a year. This may (or may not) turn out to be too gloomy; but if it happens it is by no means negligible.

The chapter on borrowing looks at this form of finance both from the lender's and from the borrower's point of view; and also contains a section on valuing debt. It also distinguishes short-term from longer-term borrowing.

There are two chapters on ordinary share capital, one mainly descriptive (though with a more analytical section on dividend policy), and the other concerned with methods of valuing equity. The fact is, of course, that it is usually extremely difficult to assess (a) what will be the future cash flows for a business, and (b) what is an appropriate discount rate to apply to those future cash flows. So it should not be surprising that valuing equity shares involves very large margins of error indeed.

Chapter 10 on corporate finance covers the tricky area of 'cost of capital'. The most difficult part of this topic is estimating the cost of equity capital; on which it would be a mistake to expect too much from financial theory. In the area of capital structure, again financial theory has failed to explain the real world very convincingly. But there is probably fairly widespread agreement that it matters more in which assets a firm invests than how it finances the investment. The section on 'The corporate life cycle' is largely based (with permission) on *Corporate Financial Strategy* by my colleague Professor Keith Ward.

This book is one of a series of texts on the 'Essence' of various business and management topics. I have tried not to overlap too much with Financial Accounting, International Finance, and so forth. Rather than only include inadequate exercises to illustrate problems, because of limits of space, I have chosen to omit them altogether. I hope I have given enough examples in the text, as a rule, to allow quantitative understanding of the points covered. Many textbook problems tend to be unrealistic because they assume that things are known for certain which in fact often have to be estimated with a very wide margin of error. Recognition of what one does not know may be the beginning of wisdom. (In teaching finance, I am often reminded of Tennyson's profound line: 'Knowledge comes but wisdom lingers.')

I would like to thank those MBA students at the Cranfield School of Management who were kind enough to comment on the book in draft form. And as usual I am very grateful to my secretary, Sheila Hart, not only for her efficiency, which I have come to take for granted, but especially for her cheerfulness and support.

1

Introduction

Business finance

Financial objectives of a business

The main **financial objective** of a business enterprise is to maximize the **wealth** of its owners. This means nearly the same as maximizing **profits**, except that measuring wealth allows for the timing of profits. Thus companies try to make profits and to avoid losses. The profit and loss account reflects success or failure in this respect.

Why are profits ever possible, above a normal rate of interest on capital invested? Essentially because of ignorance. If people dealing on markets (both buyers and sellers) already knew everything there was to be known, the prices of products would already fully reflect consumers' valuations. This **arbitrage** view of profit emphasizes the information content of price signals in the market. (Hence the destructiveness of price controls: they distort signals.)

In order to succeed in the longer term, a business must survive in the short term. Among other things, this means being able to pay its bills when they become due. Financial managers have to arrange to have cash available at the right time. The balance sheet contains details of current (short-term) assets and liabilities.

The market system

Businesses aim to make a profit by satisfying customers. It is a mistake to regard managers and workers as the two 'sides' of industry or commerce. The real distinction is between consumers on the one hand, and producers – owners, managers and workers – on the other. (Hence consumers may welcome the competition from foreign producers which domestic producers deplore.)

The market system is not a zero-sum game. If the seller makes a profit, there is no reason why the buyer must somehow *lose* to the same extent. In normal competitive markets both buyer and seller can expect to gain from voluntary market exchanges. This is because they differ in their subjective valuations of the goods or services traded. (The Greek word for 'exchange' [catallassein] also means to 'change from enmity into friendship'.) The higher the total amount of profits, the more people will have become better off as a result of market transactions. That is why, as a rule, profits are a good thing.

Consumers will not pay more than they think goods or services are worth (to them). This puts a ceiling on producers' total costs. It also gives producers an incentive to discover how much goods or services *are* worth to customers – and to find ways to add more value. Making a better or cheaper mousetrap is a good start, but consumers have to find out about it. Hence advertising is an essential part of the market system, spreading *knowledge* about new products (and reminding people about old ones).

The market economy is not static; it is a dynamic process, always having to adapt to changing conditions. The market may tend towards equilibrium, but never reaches it. New disturbing features continually appear. What has been called 'the gale of creative destruction' means long-term competition from new commodities, new technologies, new sources of supply, or new types of organiza- tion. Such basic challenges to existing products and ways of business may command a *decisive* cost or quality advantage. If so, they can strike at the very foundations of the profits and outputs of existing firms.

There are three main kinds of market in the economy: financial markets (see below); product markets, both industrial and retail; and labour markets. These deal respectively with money, goods, and people. Each is vitally important, and of course the markets are interlinked in many ways.

Owners and managers

The directors of the largest 100 UK companies between them own less than one-tenth of 1 per cent of the equity shares in their firms. With very few exceptions, they are professional managers, not owners. This gives rise to agency problems. How can principals (owners) monitor the actions of their agents (the managers), and induce them to act in the owners' interests?

Professional managers build careers on their track record of success in business. It is always open to the owners to dismiss unsuccessful managers, and hire others they hope will do better. The most important function of annual company accounts, **audited** by independent accountants, is to record the **stewardship** of managers.

It has become fashionable to reward managers partly by means of share option schemes or profit-related bonuses. But many share option schemes simply amount to methods of paying larger amounts to top managers who are already heavily committed to the success of their firms. And bonus schemes linked to reported profits may have encouraged creative (dishonest) accounting.

In contrast, owner/managers of small businesses suffer from no such potential conflict of interest. But they may not always aim to maximize their business profits. For example, the owner/manager of a small shop may prefer to close early, and not open on Saturdays, in order to enjoy more leisure. As a sole owner, he is perfectly entitled to do this if he thinks it will maximize his own psychic satisfaction. But it would hardly please the owners of a large business if its managers deliberately failed to maximize profits in order to enjoy more leisure! A competitive market would (sooner or later) replace such managers with others who *would* try to serve the owners by maximizing their wealth.

Most limited companies are private, not public ('ltd' not 'plc'). They may be too small, or too new, to meet the minimum criteria for listing. They may not need to raise more equity capital. Their main **shareholders** may not wish to realize some of their capital by selling (some of) their shares. The owner/managers may prefer to remain private, to retain control and avoid the risk of takeover. They may not relish the pressures of public **listing** – both the stock exchange regulations and the demands of investors for regular growth in earnings and dividends.

The financial environment

Financial markets

Financial markets can broadly be split between the following:

1. **Money markets**, which deal in short-term finance.

2. Foreign exchange markets, which deal in currencies (either on a spot or a forward basis).

3. **Capital markets**, which deal in long-term finance, both debt (e.g. the Eurobond market) and equity (e.g. the International Stock Exchange).

4. **Derivatives** markets, dealing in options and futures.

It is these markets which are normally open twenty-four hours a day, based on the three major centres of London, New York and Tokyo.

Financial institutions

The main private sector institutions are banks, building societies, pension funds and insurance companies. Banks are the main source of short-term and medium-term loans for businesses; while for larger firms, pension funds and insurance companies are the main source of long-term finance (both debt and equity).

The clearing banks provide for debt settlement through their system of clearing cheques and direct debits. They are also important financial **intermediaries**, receiving small amounts of savings from a large number of people and then lending them out again to individuals and businesses.

Building societies used to operate mainly by receiving deposits of savings and lending them out to enable people to buy houses and flats. (The UK's rented housing sector is smaller than it is in most other European countries.) But after deregulation of financial services in the 1980s, the larger building societies now offer a complete range of retail banking services.

Merchant (wholesale) banks arrange finance for companies (both debt and equity), and give financial advice, for example on mergers and acquisitions or on foreign currency dealing. They also manage the funds (portfolios) of pension funds, insurance companies, and investment trusts and unit trusts (see Chapter 8).

Life insurance companies and pension funds receive long-term savings from people during their working lives, often through contractual arrangements. They pay these out again, together with interest, during retirement (pensions) or on death (life assurance). (The state pension scheme is not 'funded': it runs on a 'pay-as-you-go' basis.) Partly for tax reasons, life insurance companies and pension funds have become the main owners of UK equities (see Table 1.2).

There is an important practical difference between 'defined benefit' pension schemes and 'defined contribution' schemes. At present the former are widespread. The rising stock market in the 1980s, together with 'downsizing' by many large companies, led to the pension schemes of many large employers becoming over-funded. This led to 'pension holidays' for the employers for a number of years, while the surpluses in the funds were run down. In 'defined contribution' schemes no surplus or deficit can arise in the fund: the employee simply gets whatever pension his contributions (and his employers') have earned.

In the public sector, the key financial institution is the **Bank of England**, which was founded in 1694 and nationalized in 1946. The Bank has several important functions:

1. It is the government's banker, taking in tax revenues and making payments, and managing the national debt.

2. It advises on and operates the government's monetary policy, issues bank notes and coins, and holds the country's foreign currency reserves.

3. It acts as banker for the clearing banks, and acts as lender of last resort to the financial system.

4. It supervises the banking system, and has a wider (less formal) responsibility for overseeing the financial system as a whole.

Formally the Bank of England is subordinate to the Treasury (a government department), but in practice it has a good deal of discretion. The main exception has been in the politically sensitive area of short-term interest rates. From time to time relations are somewhat strained. The Treasury is said to think of the Bank of England as its 'East End branch'; but the Bank tends to regard the Treasury as its 'West End branch'! Two recent Chancellors of the Exchequer (Nigel Lawson and Norman Lamont) have (after leaving office) revealed their support for the idea of an 'independent' Bank of England. It might have an explicit statutory duty to preserve the value of the currency – which would certainly be quite a change!

Financial sectors

The economy is split between five financial sectors: personal; industrial and commercial companies; financial institutions; government (central government, local authorities and public corporations); and overseas. Their annual financial surpluses or deficits

Table 1.1　Financial surpluses and deficits by sector, 1988–92 (£bn.)

	1988	1989	1990	1991	1992
Personal	−14	−6	+4	+18	+33
Industrial and commercial companies	−8	−22	−23	−8	−7
Financial institutions	−1	0	+3	−4	+1
	−23	−28	−16	+6	+27
Public sector					
Government	+6	+5	−2	−14	−36
Overseas sector	+17	+23	+18	+8	+9

represent the net differences between huge aggregates. Table 1.1 shows surpluses (+) and deficits (−) by sector for each of the five years 1988–92.

Table 1.2 shows the distribution of shareholding in ordinary shares of listed UK companies at five dates between 1963 and 1989. The main long-term trend is well known: between 1963 and 1989 there has been a massive switch away from personal ownership (down from 54 per cent to 21 per cent) towards pension funds (up from 6 per cent to 30 per cent). This trend has been mirrored (to a somewhat lesser extent) in the United States. And the large privatizations in the late 1980s and early 1990s have hardly interrupted it. Many of the individual subscribers to the offers for sale sold their shares within twelve months.

Accounting

The **accounts** of a company (or group of companies) consist of three main financial statements – the balance sheet; the profit and loss account; and the cash flow statement (see Chapter 3) – together with the notes to the accounts and the auditors' report.

Balance sheet

The **balance sheet** shows a firm's financial position as at the end of an accounting period. It classifies items between assets (*uses* of funds) and liabilities (*sources* of funds). Table 1.3 sets out a simple example of a balance sheet.

Table 1.2 Shareholdings in ordinary shares of UK listed companies in 1963, 1969, 1975, 1981, and 1989 (%) (Source: Central Statistical Office, Share Register Survey Report, end 1989, Table 2)

	1963	1969	1975	1981	1989
Personal					
Persons	54.0	47.4	37.5	28.2	21.3
Charities	2.1	2.1	2.3	2.2	2.0
	56.1	49.5	39.8	30.4	23.3
Industrial and commercial					
companies	5.1	5.4	3.0	5.1	3.6
Financial institutions					
Pension funds	6.4	9.1	16.8	26.7	30.4
Insurance companies	10.0	12.2	15.9	20.5	18.4
Unit trusts	1.3	2.9	4.1	3.6	5.9
Investment trusts and other	11.3	10.1	10.5	6.8	3.2
Banks	1.3	1.7	0.7	0.3	0.9
	30.3	36.0	48.0	57.9	58.8
Public sector	1.5	2.6	3.6	3.0	2.0
Overseas	7.0	6.6	5.6	3.6	12.4
TOTAL	100.0	100.0	100.0	100.0	100.0

An **asset** is a valuable resource controlled by a business. Assets are usually stated at original (historical) **cost,** less any deductions to allow for subsequent using-up or erosion of value. **Fixed assets** are long-term resources used to provide goods or services, rather than to be sold in the normal course of business. They include land, buildings, equipment and vehicles. **Current assets** are short-term resources likely to be turned into cash within twelve months from the balance sheet date. The three main current assets appear in reverse order of liquidity: stocks, debtors, cash.

A **liability** is money a business owes to others. **Current liabilities** are due for payment within at most twelve months from the balance sheet date. They are usually deducted from total current assets, to produce a total for **working capital** (= net current assets).

Total assets less current liabilities (£1,500,000 for Hardstaff Engineering Limited) represents net long-term uses of funds (**net assets**) which must be financed by long-term sources of funds (**capital employed**).

Table 1.3   Hardstaff Engineering Ltd: balance sheet as at 31 March 1994

	£'000	£'000
Fixed assets:		
Intangible		200
Tangible		550
Investments		100
		850
Current assets:		
Stocks	450	
Debtors	400	
Cash	150	
	1,000	
Less: Current liabilities	350	
Working capital		650
Total assets *less* current liabilities		1,500
Less: Long-term liabilities		300
		1,200
Shareholders' funds:		
Called-up ordinary share capital		500
Retained profits		700
		1,200

Long-term liabilities are amounts borrowed which are repayable more than twelve months from the balance sheet date. Regular interest payments are due on the amounts owing.

Shareholders' funds are amounts provided directly or indirectly by the owners of the business, shown under the heading 'capital and **reserves**'. They may be regarded as ultimate liabilities of a company to its shareholders. But as long as the company continues in business no amounts are legally payable, unless the directors decide to distribute dividends out of profits. Shareholders provide called-up share capital directly, by paying the company cash for **ordinary shares** in the business. Shares in listed companies can be bought and sold on the Stock Exchange. **Retained profits** are provided indirectly: they represent profits earned by a business (and attributed to shareholders in the balance sheet) which have not been paid out in dividends.

The amount of long-term sources of funds necessarily equals long-term net uses of funds. Hence balance sheets always balance! This is the famous principle of **double-entry accounting**, which Goethe called: 'The finest invention of the human mind'.

The **vertical format** first deducts current liabilities from current assets, and then deducts long-term liabilities from the subtotal of total assets less current liabilities. For Hardstaff Engineering Ltd, the three kinds of sources of funds are:

	£'000
Current liabilities	350
Long-term liabilities	300
Shareholders' funds	1,200
	1,850

In total, of course, they equal total uses of funds (assets):

	£'000
Fixed assets	850
Current assets	1,000
	1,850

Profit and loss account

The **profit and loss account** (P & L account) summarizes a firm's income and expenses for a period (normally a year). It shows how much profit has been paid in **dividends** to shareholders, the balance of profit for the period being retained in the business (and representing the *link* with the balance sheet).

Profit is **sales revenue** (turnover) less total **expenses** for a period; and a **loss** is simply a negative profit. As Table 1.4 shows, much of the detail in a profit and loss account consists of a classified list of the various expenses, with subtotals at intervals. A published profit

Table 1.4 Hardstaff Engineering Ltd: profit and loss account for the year ended 31 March 1994

	£'000	£'000
Turnover		2,400
Cost of sales:		
Depreciation	150	
Other costs	1,550	
	——	1,700
		——
Gross profit		700
Selling and distribution costs	170	
Administrative expenses	290	
	——	460
		——
Operating profit		240
Interest payable		40
		——
Profit before tax		200
Tax on profit		50
		——
Profit after tax		150
Ordinary dividends		60
		——
Retained profit for the year		90
		——

and loss account would normally show in the notes the details of operational expenses in the box.

To help run the business, however, internal ('management') accounts would show much more, both for the balance sheet and the profit and loss account. For example:

1. Results for periods shorter than a year, often one month.
2. Results analyzed by product group or geographically or both.
3. **Budgets** for future periods, as well as past results.
4. Much more detailed analysis for income and expenses and for assets and liabilities.

One way to assess business performance is by looking at **value added** – the difference between sales revenue (turnover) and the cost of bought-in goods and services. It is roughly equivalent to profit (before interest and tax) plus wages. Total national output (gross domestic product) is determined by adding together the value added of all the firms in the economy (*not* their sales revenues, which would involve considerable double-counting).

Basic accounting concepts

Four basic accounting concepts underlie the figures in any set of accounts:

1. The **going concern** concept assumes that an enterprise will continue in business for the foreseeable future. This normally means accounts showing assets at (recoverable) *cost*. If one assumed that the firm was about to be wound up (liquidated), it would then be prudent to show assets at the amount they would realize on immediate sale (**net realizable value**), which might be much *less* than cost.

2. The **accruals** concept where possible **matches** expenses against revenues: firms recognize revenues as they earn them and expenses as they incur them in transactions. It would normally be less realistic for a firm to recognize transactions only when it received or paid *cash*. (The British government has recently announced that it is (finally!) going to switch from cash accounting to accrual accounting.)

3. The **consistency** concept requires the same accounting treatment for similar items from one period to another, to allow readers to compare results between periods. Any deviations should be disclosed and quantified.

4. The **prudence** concept means that accounts include revenues and profits only when they are **realized**, either in cash or in the form of assets whose ultimate proceeds are fairly certain. In contrast, accounts provide in full for all expected losses and expenses even where their amount has to be estimated.

The basic purpose of accounts is to show a **true and fair view** of a firm's financial position and profit or loss for the period. The balance sheet does not try to show a firm's current value (so the American expression 'net worth' in balance sheets to refer to the interests of shareholders is misleading). Accounts exclude many important assets, especially internally generated assets, such as business knowhow.

Return on investment

A common measure of operating performance is return on investment in net assets. This may be called:

- Return on investment (ROI).
- Return on net assets (RONA).
- Return on capital employed (ROCE).
- Return on funds employed (ROFE).

This important ratio expresses operating profit (**profit before interest and tax**) as a percentage of long-term net operating assets, either for the whole company or for parts of it. A firm can compare how profitably it employs its assets against the returns available from other possible uses of scarce capital funds.

For Hardstaff Engineering Limited, the return on net assets for the year ended 31 March 1994 was 16.0 per cent:

$$\frac{\text{Operating profit}}{\text{Net assets}} = \frac{240}{1,500} = 16.0 \text{ per cent}$$

This can also be expressed as profit margin × net asset turnover:

$$\frac{\text{Operating profit}}{\text{Sales}} = \frac{240}{2,400} = 10.0 \text{ per cent}$$

$$\frac{\text{Sales}}{\text{Net assets}} = \frac{2,400}{1,500} = 1.6 \text{ times}$$

Profit margin 10.0 per cent × net asset turnover 1.6 times = 16.0 per cent.

Another useful way to analyze a company's rate of return on net assets is to set out the main items of profit and net assets in a diagram, as in Figure 1.1. The main components of operating profit (sales revenue, cost of materials, cost of labour, overheads) can each be analyzed between *quantity* and *price*; and this basic approach will often give useful clues to possible improvements.

In general, to improve its rate of return on net assets, a company can either increase its profit for a given amount of net assets, or maintain its operating profit while reducing the amount of net assets employed. It can then invest any surplus capital to earn a return, and thus increase total profits.

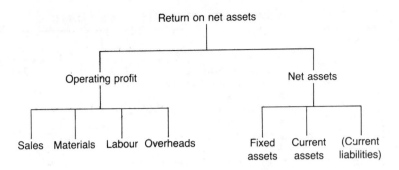

Figure 1.1   Analysis of return on net assets

An alternative way to view return on investment is to deduct from the return a charge representing interest on all capital employed. Anything left may be regarded as close to true economic profit: it is called **residual income (RI)**, or **economic value added (EVA)**. If Hardstaff Engineering, for example, used a capital charge of 15 per cent (before tax), the amount of residual income would be:

	£'000
Operating profit	240
Less: Capital charge: 15 per cent × 1,500	225
Residual income	+15

Evidently it would be possible for companies reporting a positive accounting profit to show a negative residual income (in other words, an economic *loss*) if their accounting profit was not high enough to cover the capital charge.

Accounting standards

Company accounts are required to give 'a true and fair view' of the state of affairs as at the end of the financial year, and of the profit or loss for the financial year. There are two main sources of rules instructing accountants how to achieve this: company law, as expressed in the Companies Act 1985 (as amended in 1989), and **accounting standards**.

Company law is now heavily influenced by the European Com-

Table 1.5 UK Accounting Standards as at 30 September 1994

Disclosure			
SSAP	2	Accounting Policies	1971
SSAP	3	Earnings Per Share	1972, 1984
SSAP	17	Post Balance Sheet Events	1980
SSAP	18	Contingencies	1980
SSAP	25	Segmental Reporting	1990
FRS	1	Cash Flow Statements	1991
FRS	3	Reporting Financial Performance	1992
FRS	4	Capital Instruments	1993
FRS	5	The Substance of Transactions	1994
Tax			
SSAP	4	Government Grants	1974, 1990
SSAP	5	Value Added Tax	1974
SSAP	8	Tax Under the Imputation System	1974, 1977
SSAP	15	Deferred Tax	1978, 1985
Groups			
SSAP	1	Associated Companies	1971, 1982
SSAP	20	Foreign Currency Translation	1983
SSAP	22	Goodwill	1984
FRS	2	Subsidiary Undertakings	1992
FRS	6	Acquisitions and Mergers	1994
FRS	7	Fair Values on Acquisition	1994
Miscellaneous			
SSAP	9	Stocks and Work in Progress	1975, 1988
SSAP	12	Depreciation	1977, 1987
SSAP	13	Research and Development	1977, 1989
SSAP	19	Investment Properties	1981
SSAP	21	Leases and Hire Purchase Contracts	1984
SSAP	24	Pension Costs	1988

Note: SSAPs refer to Statements of Standard Accounting Practice, issued between 1971 and 1990 by the Accounting Standards Committee. FRSs refer to Financial Reporting Standards, issued since 1990 by the Accounting Standards Board.

munity, in particular the Fourth and Seventh Directives which set out required formats for accounts, and rules about group accounts. Schedules 4 and 5 to the Companies Act 1985, covering the form and content of company accounts and the notes thereto, amount to no less than fifty pages.

The twenty-five UK accounting standards contain even more detailed instructions, comprising, with notes, more than 600 pages in all! Table 1.5 lists the topics covered, grouped under four headings: disclosure; tax; groups; and miscellaneous. The Accounting Standards Board says: 'Accounting standards are authoritative statements of how particular types of transaction and other events should be reflected in financial statements and accordingly compliance with accounting standards will normally be necessary for financial statements to give a true and fair view.' This assertion has not yet been tested in the courts.

Problems in finance

Time

The difference between the near and distant future is important in finance, as in other areas of business. Long-term investments may involve **expenditures** promising returns only after many years; while long-term borrowing can provide funds which are safe because they need not be repaid for a long time.

A business may often choose to sacrifice a smaller profit soon in the hope of a larger profit later: for example, pricing low with a new product in order to build up market share. Maximizing the wealth of the firm's owners requires some way to compare profits in different future periods. This is done by using the rate of interest, in effect, as an 'exchange rate through time' (see Chapter 2). Trying to forecast cash receipts and payments in the uncertain future involves not only the *amount* of cash flows, but also their *timing*.

In general, firms often try to **match** the **maturities** of their liabilities (sources of finance) with those of their assets (uses of funds). So do financial institutions. 'Borrowing short and lending long' can clearly be dangerous (risky): a firm might then have to repay the borrowings at short notice without being able to demand repayment of its own long-term investments.

Uncertainty

The future is uncertain. Hence financial plans, like others, may go wrong. Financial managers try to allow sufficient margin of error to cover most risks, without playing it so safe that little profit remains. But (as the Bible says), 'time and chance happeneth to them all' [Ecclesiastes 9:11].

It is usual to distinguish between **risk** and **uncertainty**. The term 'risk' is used where the chance of each possible outcome is known (as in roulette or with dice). Uncertainty exists when – as is usual in business – one can only estimate the odds subjectively (that is, guess). (This topic is discussed further in Chapter 6.) For example, business uncertainty is likely to be high in the following circumstances where:

1. A firm is heavily dependent on a single product line, or a single customer.
2. Market conditions make accurate sales forecasts difficult; this may be due either to unpredictable changes in customers' tastes (in businesses subject to vagaries of fashion) or to competitive pressures.
3. Technical changes are affecting the industry's cost structure.
4. Senior managers change, especially if several go at once.
5. Government policies change.

Liquidity

Liquidity means the ease with which an owner can turn an asset into cash: both the speed and the certainty of net proceeds. In a perfect capital market this would not matter, since an asset's owner would always be able to borrow its full value. But in the real world it may often be easier to turn cash into assets than assets into cash.

As usual, financial managers need to seek a *balance*. Having too little liquidity might lead to problems in paying bills; while having too much might result in a low rate of return. Rule-of-thumb measures of liquidity can be misleading (see Chapter 4).

Gearing

The two main forms of finance are ordinary shareholders' funds ('equity') and borrowing ('debt'). They are discussed in detail in Chapters 8 and 9. When borrowing forms a large proportion of its total capital structure, a company is 'highly geared'. In Chapter 10 we note some rules of thumb about how much financial **gearing** a firm can take on without undue alarm.

Financial gearing (financial risk) refers to the sources of a company's finance; operational gearing (business risk) refers to the nature of the business and how a firm has used its funds. How a firm invests funds is probably far more important than its sources of finance. This is because most financial markets are more competitive, with better information, than most factor markets dealing in 'real' goods and services. So, in general, financing decisions provide fewer chances of significant profit or loss.

'Operational gearing' sometimes refers to the level of fixed expenses as a proportion of total expenses. Thus most of a school's expenses are fixed, whereas most of a street trader's are variable. Where most expenses are fixed, the amount of profit is very sensitive to the level of sales revenue. (The marginal cost of supplying one more student in a school is normally very small; so almost all that student's tuition fee represents profit!)

Inflation

Inflation causes problems which are both important and complicated; and any rate of inflation above three or four per cent a year is serious. Inflation affects the following factors:

1. The required rates of return on new investments.
2. The valuation of assets.
3. The management of working capital.
4. The proper extent and type of borrowing.
5. Foreign exchange rates.
6. The accuracy of accounts using money as the unit of measurement.

In discussing financial numbers, we must be careful to distinguish between 'money' ('nominal') amounts and '**real**' amounts (expressed in terms of constant purchasing power). Another critical question is whether or not a particular rate of inflation was *anticipated*. (It is unanticipated inflation that can be especially damaging.) We must also consider possible fluctuations in the inflation rate over time.

Tax

Businesses are subject to many taxes – on sales, on wages, on property, on capital. But business finance mainly deals with only three kinds of tax:

1. Corporation tax (CT) on a firm's 'taxable profits'.

2. Personal income tax on dividends to shareholders.

3. Capital gains tax (CGT) on increases in the value of equity shares.

A business which aims to maximize owners' wealth has to calculate the tax effects on individuals. But it should try to maximize after-tax profits, not to minimize taxes. Inflation complicates the impact of tax, since (either by accident or design) the tax system may not always properly allow for it. Hence there are some distortions which affect both the sources of finance and investment projects.

2

Interest rates

Interest rates can allow us to compare money amounts at different points in time. This is crucial in business (and in economics generally). The **interest rate** consists of three component parts: time preference, inflation premium, and risk premium.

Time

Pure time preference

Pure **time preference** refers to the ratio between how consumers value present goods as against the same goods in future. If consumers did not in general prefer present goods to future goods, they would never consume anything! The convention is to quote the ratio as an annual rate. In effect, a pure interest rate represents the 'price of time'. It need not relate to *money*, though it often does.

People used to talk about firms trying to 'maximize profits'. Modern finance theory talks about 'maximizing wealth'. This allows for the *timing* of profits (or cash flows? – see Chapter 3) – which matters to owners (and therefore to managers).

The term structure of interest rates

The different maturity dates of UK government securities ('gilts') reveal the **term structure** of interest rates. That means how annual rates of interest vary depending on the length of time until a loan has to be repaid.

Charting interest yields against the time to **maturity** may show at least three different shapes (see Figure 2.1). The 'slope' reads from left to right, that is from short-term to long-term. According to the *expectations* theory, the term structure will be upwards-sloping if investors expect that interest rates will rise, but downwards-sloping if they expect interest rates to fall. An important influence may be expected future rates of *inflation* (see below). The *liquidity preference* theory argues that most lenders want to lend short-term, while most borrowers want to borrow long-term. Hence borrowers have to offer lenders a premium, to induce them to lend long, which implies an upward-sloping term structure. This may reflect an aspect of *risk* (see below).

Index-linked gilts

The British government recently started issuing **index-linked** gilts, securities which are guaranteed against inflation. Government securities are normally regarded as risk-free, in that a government which controls the printing presses is almost certain to be willing and able to repay any money it has borrowed. (The **inflation premium** which lenders may demand reflects the possibility that the purchasing power of the money repaid may be less than the purchasing power of the money originally lent.)

The yield on index-linked gilts thus provides direct market measure of 'pure' time-preference. In June 1994 (varying slightly, depending on the term), index-linked gilts yielded nearly 4 per cent a year. This compares with a somewhat lower rate – about 2.5 per cent – throughout most of the nineteenth century. (In those days there was no expectation of continuous inflation, hence nominal **yields** on risk-free gilts were also equivalent to 'real' yields.)

The rate of pure time-preference, like other market prices, can vary over time; though much more important reasons for interest rates to vary are inflation and risk, to which we now turn.

Inflation

The inflation premium

Rates of interest on money include an inflation premium. As the name implies, this allows for the expected future rate of inflation of

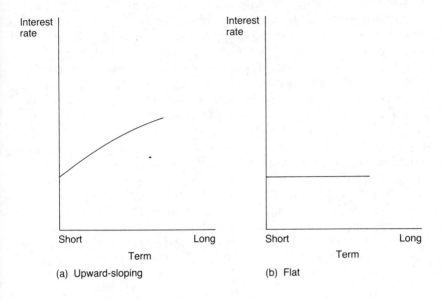

(a) Upward-sloping   (b) Flat

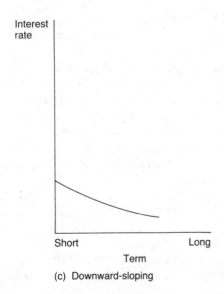

(c) Downward-sloping

Figure 2.1   Three kinds of 'term structure' of interest rates

the currency concerned. The yield on ordinary British government securities is much higher now than it was a century ago, because inflation is (expected to be) much higher now. For the same reason, money interest rates are much higher in Brazil than in Switzerland because people expect higher inflation in Brazil.

If the interest rate would be 4 per cent a year in the absence of inflation, and if both borrower and lender expect future inflation of 6 per cent a year, then the nominal money rate of interest will be about 10 per cent a year. (Strictly it should be not $4 + 6 = 10$ per cent, but $1.06 \times 1.04 = 1.1024$, or 10.24 per cent.)

Of course, people may be wrong about the future rate of inflation. In the 1970s, nominal interest rates were much lower than the rate of inflation turned out to be. So 'real' interest rates (money interest rates minus actual rates of inflation) were negative.

In June 1994, for 15-year maturities money gilts yielded nearly 9 per cent, index-linked gilts nearly 4 per cent. Hence the market seemed to expect UK inflation over the next fifteen years to average about 5 per cent a year. (That would halve the purchasing power of money over the period.)

Inflation and the term structure

Long-term inflation expectations may be slow to change. Just before sterling left the exchange rate mechanism (ERM) of the European Monetary System in September 1992, the short-term UK interest rate stood at about 10 per cent a year. This may have seemed rather high in the depth of a recession, with inflation at 3½ per cent a year and falling. But the rate was thought necessary to keep sterling within the agreed ERM band. In particular, high UK interest rates were required to match high German interest rates, which were intended to control German inflation.

When it proved impossible to keep sterling within the ERM, the British Chancellor of the Exchequer started 'singing in his bath'. UK short-term interest rates fell to around 6 per cent very soon – more suitable for the domestic UK economy when sterling was no longer tied at a fixed rate to the Deutschmark. Longer-term UK interest rates, however, scarcely moved. So a downward-sloping term structure at the end of August (expecting interest rates to fall from their short-term level) was replaced by an upward-sloping term structure at the end of September (now expecting interest rates to rise from their much-reduced short-term level).

UK post-war inflation

There have been three main eras of inflation in the post-war period in the UK:

1. Moderate for the fifteen years 1953–67 (average rate about 3 per cent a year).
2. High for the fourteen years 1968–81 (average rate about 12 per cent a year).
3. Lower for the twelve years 1982–93 (average rate about 5 per cent a year).

Five per cent a year *cumulative* is hardly negligible. It reduces the **purchasing power** of money by 97½ per cent over a lifetime of seventy-five years (in other words, over that period prices on average multiply fortyfold).

Figure 2.2 shows the cumulative impact of **currency debasement** on the value of government securities (2½ per cent Consolidated Stock) over the post-war years. The notorious issue of 'Dalton's', carrying a coupon rate of 2½ per cent, was made *at par* in 1946. By June 1994 the *money* price was 29, and (in terms of 1946 purchasing power) each £100 nominal of stock was worth about £1.50. This does highlight the point that even 'risk-free' securities are not completely safe from loss if there is inflation.

Figure 2.3 shows the fifteen-year average annual rates of UK inflation between 1967 and 1993. Until after the Second World War the fifteen-year annual average rate of inflation had never exceeded 2 per cent a year in peacetime. Indeed, as far as one can tell, the purchasing power of the pound was much the same on the outbreak of the First World War in 1914 as it had been on the Restoration of Charles II in 1660. In other words, over quarter of a millennium between those two dates the UK currency had been virtually stable.

This background helps one understand that the double-digit rates of inflation common during the 1970s (worldwide, not just in the UK) were completely unprecedented. It is perhaps not surprising that some important financial institutions (in particular the tax system and accounting standards) reacted slowly if at all.

The normal convention in **financial accounting** is to use historical money costs. Two alternative approaches have been used in times of rapid inflation. **Constant purchasing power (CPP)** accounting continues to use historical costs, but indexes money costs (by means of an index of general inflation) into terms of constant purchasing

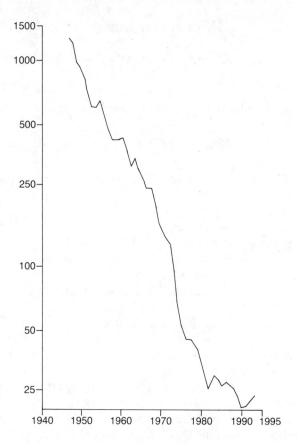

Figure 2.2   The real value of 2½ per cent Consolidated Stock, 1946–93, in
constant January 1987 pounds.

power. **Current cost accounting (CCA)** continues to use money as
the unit of account, but uses the estimated replacement cost of
assets (as a rule) instead of the actual historical cost. In the UK,
accounting standards were issued first for CPP (SSAP 7), then for
CCA (SSAP 16); but both were soon withdrawn. The decline in the
rate of inflation has led to a loss of momentum for change.

Inflation and foreign exchange rates

The **purchasing power parity** (PPP) theorem states that – in the
long-run – foreign exchange rates will adjust to reflect the relative

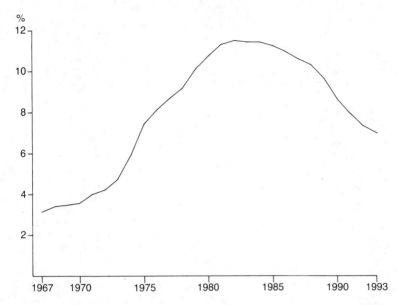

Figure 2.3 Fifteen-year average annual rates of UK inflation, 1967–93

rates of inflation of the currencies concerned. This explains, for example, why the pound sterling has fallen as much as it has against the German Deutschmark, as shown in Figure 2.4.

In 1969 the pound was equivalent to DM 8.84, whereas by 1991 it was worth only DM 2.93. The average rate of inflation in Germany over the twenty-two-year period was about 4½ per cent a year, compared with about 10 per cent a year in the United Kingdom. Hence the exchange rate of sterling fell against the Deutschmark by an average of about 5 per cent a year between 1969 and 1991. (One has to pick both the starting date and the finishing date carefully to get such an apparently accurate result!)

Turning this theorem around helps to explain the tensions within the ERM over foreign exchange rates. If these are to be fixed, it follows that long-run rates of inflation must be the same in all the European countries. But this implies – virtually – a Community-wide economic policy. Some of the political consequences of this are not necessarily welcome. A British politician pointed out that it might be difficult to convince a regional audience in the United Kingdom of the need for heavy unemployment in order to implement the Bundesbank's monetary policy.

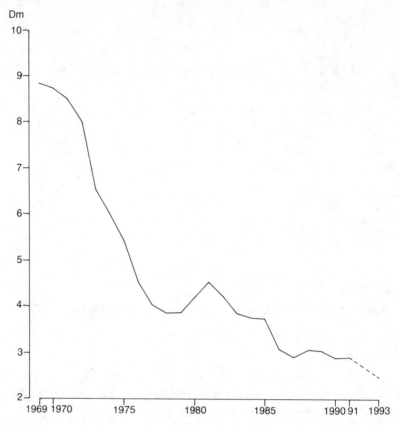

Figure 2.4 The pound sterling against the German Deutschmark, 1969–93

Risk and required return

Risk premium

The third component in most interest rates on business loans is a **risk premium**. Smaller businesses often have to pay a higher rate of interest than large ones because lending to them is usually 'riskier'. This means that smaller firms in general are more likely to default on interest or principal repayments. Rather than require an extremely high-risk premium, a bank which thinks the risk very large may

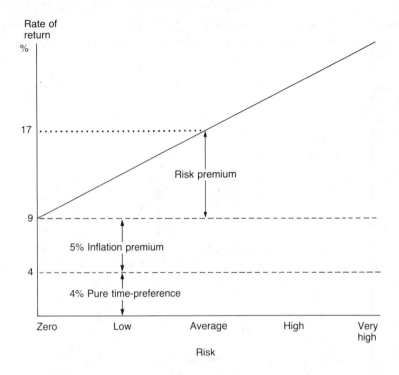

Figure 2.5 Risk and required return

simply refuse to lend at all. Risk may relate to the nature of the business, rather than its size. For example, food retailing is normally regarded as relatively stable, whereas drilling for oil is notoriously risky.

Modern portfolio theory (discussed in more detail in Chapter 9) suggests a straight-line relationship between 'risk' (suitably defined) and a lender's required rate of return. This implies a similar straight-line relationship between the risk premium demanded and the level of risk.

The 'capital market line' in Figure 2.5 shows this. Even at *zero* risk, there is still a positive interest rate of 9 per cent, which represents pure time-preference of 4 per cent plus an inflation premium of 5 per cent. Thus the yield on 'risk-free' government securities would be 4 per cent on index-linked gilts, and 9 per cent on ordinary money gilts. (Note that taxation is ignored here.) Thereafter as risk increases (reading from left to right, along the horizontal axis) so does the return required on the vertical axis. For an investment involving 'average risk', a risk premium of 8 per cent is required.

(How this is derived is explained in Chapter 8.) Thus the total required rate of return for an average-risk investment is 17 per cent, made up as follows:

	%
Pure time-preference	4
Inflation premium	5
Average risk premium	8
Total required rate of return	17

It will be obvious that the required rate of return could be very different for a low-risk or a high-risk project, or for an investment in a currency other than sterling, where inflation expectations were different.

Short-termism

Do business managers take too **'short-term'** a view of the future? Perhaps their pay depends too much on short-term accounting results. This might mean they overlook longer-term benefits altogether (as with their widespread use of the payback method of capital project appraisal) or that companies, in effect, use too *high* a discount rate in 'valuing' the future (see Chapter 5). Some cynical definitions certainly have a 'short-termist' flavour, for example: 'A long-term investment is a short-term investment that has gone wrong.'

Market prices set the yields for government (risk-free) securities, which comprise pure time-preference plus an inflation premium. Hence there is little room for disagreement about them. So perhaps companies are using too high a risk premium for capital projects? Risk assessment, by its nature, is subjective. Managers may be using a risk premium which tries to allow for total risk, rather than just 'specific' risk (which modern portfolio theory would suggest: see Chapter 9).

If the stock market values shares on the basis of future dividends (see Chapter 9), with current gross **dividend yields** of 4 per cent, then expected cash receipts to shareholders in the first five years represent less than 20 per cent of the market price of most shares. In other words, more than 80 per cent of the current market price depends on cash flows more than five years ahead. That does not, on the face of it, seem too short-termist.

In contrast, governments notoriously find it hard to see beyond the next election – which, on average, is only about two years ahead. It was Harold Wilson who said, 'A week is a long time in politics' – the quintessential short-termist view of a politician!

3

Cash

Uses of cash

What is money?

Money is any generally accepted medium of exchange. Its main function is to act as a means of payment. If there were no money people would have to exchange goods and services by means of barter. This is a cumbersome process, where two people must each want precisely what the other has got.

Centuries ago, gold or silver came to serve as money, being relatively scarce, stable, durable, divisible, and easy to recognize. The ruler's seal on a coin stated and guaranteed its weight (and implied its fineness); this avoided the need to assay or weigh the metal at each payment, and made such coins acceptable 'at face value'. Eventually milled edges prevented coin-clipping; but rulers of nations themselves often 'debased' coins by adding base metal to the precious metal.

Bankers held money (gold) in safe-keeping and issued paper notes (receipts) to the owners (depositors). These banknotes represented a promise to pay the holder on demand a certain amount (weight) of gold, and most people found them convenient to use for payments. Soon, therefore, bankers saw no need to 'back' each paper note with equivalent gold in their vaults. In practice a bank could issue about ten times more 'paper money' than the gold it held, and lend out the extra money at interest to borrowers.

Some loans would be for *long* periods; so if every holder of a bank's paper notes were to demand instant repayment in gold (a 'run on the bank'), the bank would be unable by a wide margin to meet its legal obligations. Hence prudent banks had to take great care to avoid any loss of public confidence in their **solvency**. They did this partly by matching the maturities of their assets and liabilities and partly by very cautious attitudes towards risk. As a result the paper notes of a reliable bank were reckoned to be 'as good as gold'.

In time central banks evolved, to serve as banker to the government as well as to the commercial banks. They often became the sole issuer of paper notes and 'lenders of last resort' (see Chapter 1). Eventually most governments nationalized their central banks, and withdrew people's right to convert paper banknotes into gold. That made it easy (and tempting) for governments to go on printing more and more notes, thus inflating the supply of paper ('fiat') currency.

The quantity theory of money, in its simplest form, says that the larger the money supply, the less the value (purchasing power) of each unit of currency. Keynes accepted that in the long run this was probably true; but famously said that 'in the long run we are all dead'. One of the main practical problems of business management is balancing the short-term and the long-term.

A stable money can represent a store of wealth. More important, as long as the purchasing power of money is reasonably stable, it can represent a **unit of account**. This allows economic calculation in terms of money. If money loses purchasing power fast, however (as in modern times), it becomes less useful as a unit of account; hence pressures for a system of **inflation accounting** (see Chapter 2).

Why do firms need cash?

Most people carry some cash around with them to cover various day-to-day transactions, such as paying for a haircut or a bus fare. In the same way, firms may need large sums of money, for example, to pay weekly wages or, from time to time, to pay for new equipment, to settle tax bills, or to repay borrowing.

But carrying too much cash can be risky. There are sometimes reports of mysterious Nigerians carrying £250,000 around London in used notes who stop for a cup of coffee and when they emerge find their taxi has disappeared with their cash in a bag on the back seat. Banknotes – being anonymous – are subject to the risk of loss; but this does not apply to cash held in a bank account.

Strictly speaking, what is needed is not so much cash itself as the 'ability to pay'. Thus many individuals now carry credit cards to let them make day-to-day purchases for which they might once have needed cash. In the same way, a firm which has arranged **bank overdraft** facilities may not need to hold any positive cash balance with its bank: it can simply continue to draw cheques up to the extent of its borrowing limit.

Many retail shops hold quite large sums of cash in their tills. This is not to cover cash purchases (for which they would use other sources); nor is it merely a result of cash takings from sales (which they would promptly bank). The main function of till cash is to enable shops to offer change to customers paying in cash. An old cartoon joke shows a passenger apologizing to a bus conductor as he offers a £50 note in payment of a £1 bus fare: 'I'm afraid I haven't got any change.' The conductor pours 490 10p pieces into his lap and replies: 'Well, you have now!'

The pattern of weekly cash receipts and payments in most businesses will fluctuate somewhat. For example, bad weather may reduce cash sales of a department store. A firm may choose to hold some extra cash to be on the safe side, so that even if things go slightly wrong, it will still be able to make ends meet. The amount of the cash safety margin will depend on how business managers feel about the risks of running out of cash (both how likely it is, and how much it would matter). A firm may also happen to hold cash as a result of errors in forecasts of the timing or amount of cash receipts or payments. (Governments may happen to be overdrawn for the same reason!)

Finally the speculative motive is ever-present in business. Stock exchange investors may increase their cash holdings by selling shares whose price they expect to fall. To succeed (in making a profit) they must guess not just the *direction* in which the market is going to move, but also the timing. (I knew a far-sighted investor who realized as early as 1938 that the fixed $35 per ounce price of gold would have to increase sooner or later, as a result of cumulative American inflation. Unfortunately not until 1968 – thirty years later – was he proved correct.) Similar motives may underlie changes in cash holdings in many firms, for example where they expect raw materials prices to change.

Flows of cash in business

A firm gets money from three main sources:

1. Owners, who start the business with equity share capital (and sometimes contribute more share capital later).

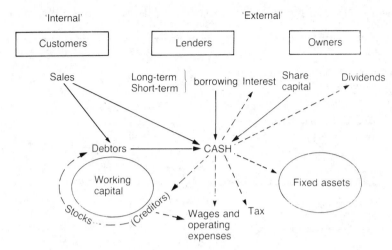

Figure 3.1 Main flows of funds

2. Lenders (banks and others), who provide long-term or short-term funds.
3. Customers, in respect of goods or services sold to them.

Funds deriving from sales to customers are sometimes referred to as **internal finance**, funds from owners or lenders as **external finance**.

A business spends money on three main kinds of thing:

1. Long-term ('fixed') assets, such as buildings and equipment.
2. Short-term ('current') assets, such as stocks of materials.
3. Wages and other current expenses.

Figure 3.1 shows the major sources and uses of funds in business, including the payment of cash dividends.

Cash flow statement

In addition to the profit and loss account and the balance sheet, all but small companies must also publish a cash flow statement. ('Small' companies are defined roughly as those with annual turnover under £2 million or total assets under £1 million or fewer than 50 employees.) Table 3.1 shows, somewhat simplified, the format of the cash flow statement.

'Cash' includes 'cash equivalents', which are defined as short-term highly liquid investments that are readily convertible into

Table 3.1 Hardstaff Engineering Ltd: cash flow statement for the year ended 31 March 1994

	£'000	£'000
Operating		
Operating profit before tax and interest		240
Add: Depreciation		150
		390
Less: Increase in working capital:		
(Debtors up)	(40)	(60)
(Stocks up)	(35)	—
Creditors up	15	
Cash generated from operations		330
Less: Interest paid	(40)	
Tax paid	(40)	
Dividends paid	(50)	
	(130)*	
Net cash from operations		200
Investing		
Purchase of tangible fixed assets	(130)	
Proceeds from sale of tangible fixed assets	10	
Acquisition of subsidiary	(70)	
		(190)
Financing		
Proceeds from issuing ordinary shares	10	
Proceeds from long-term borrowing	40	
		50
Net increase in cash		60

Note: *Showable under operations under the international accounting standard IAS 7, but separately under the UK standard FRS 1.

known amounts of cash and that were within three months of maturity when acquired.

A steady-state company should be able to finance replacement of tangible fixed assets out of net cash from operations. (In the absence of cumulative inflation, one might expect net spending on tangible fixed assets roughly to equal the provision for depreciation.) But an expanding company may not only acquire new subsidiaries from time to time; but may also increase its capacity by purchase of fixed assets. This may require external financing, either by debt or equity.

'Free cash flow' represents net cash generated over and above the level of reinvestment required to 'maintain' the scale of activity in future. In practice it is rarely possible to measure how much spending on fixed assets is for 'replacement' and how much represents 'expansion'.

In a balance sheet, 'Cash' (sometimes '**liquid resources**') normally comprises three items:

1. Cash in hand, which consists of notes and coins. Accountants call it 'petty cash', and in most businesses the total is not significant.
2. Current accounts with banks (demand deposits), available to make payments by cheque, or to draw out in cash (for example, to pay wages in cash). Such accounts often do not earn interest.
3. Deposit accounts with banks (time deposits), which do earn interest; and can be converted into cash on short notice (often seven days).

Another category in balance sheets under current assets is 'marketable securities'. These may include investments which count as 'cash equivalents' under the FRS 1 definition; for practical purposes, they are often very similar to cash.

Cash and profit

Cash and profit are different

Cash and profit are two of the main concerns of the financial manager. Both are important, but they are different. Cash is a liquid asset owned by a business, enabling it to buy goods or services. A firm's cash balance can be either *too large* (earning a low rate of return) or too small (risky). Profit is an accounting measure of the surplus earned after deducting all business expenses from sales revenues and other income for a period. In general, the larger the profit the better. Table 3.2 lists and classifies some of the main differences between cash and profit.

In accrual accounting, the amount of expenses in a period will usually not equal the amount of cash paid out. Where a company acquires tangible fixed assets for cash, it does not deduct the whole

Table 3.2.   Why profit and cash may differ

Difference	Balance sheet effect
1. P & L expense, not cash payment	Profit *down*
• Purchase on credit	Creditors *up*
• Tax charge not yet paid	Tax liability *up*
• Depreciation of fixed asset	Net fixed assets *down*
• Write off bad debt or stock	Debtors or stock *down*
2. Cash payment, not P & L expense	Cash *down*
• Purchase of long-term asset, for cash	Fixed assets *up*
• Purchase of stock, for cash	Stock *up*
• Dividend paid	Equity *down*
• Payment of creditor	Liability *down*
3. P & L income, not cash receipt	Profit *up*
• Sale on credit	Debtors *up*
• Reduce provision for expense	Provisions (liabilities) *down*
• Share of subsidiary/associate profit	Investment *up*
4. Cash receipt, not P & L income	Cash *up*
• Sale of fixed asset, for cash	Fixed assets *down*
• Debtors settle account	Debtors *down*
• Borrow long-term loan	Loans *up*
• Issue share capital, for cash	Equity *up*

cost from profit in the same period. Instead the firm's accounts charge only a fraction of the cost as **depreciation** expense in each period of the asset's life. If a firm sells goods for more than they cost, it has made a profit. But until the customers have paid for the goods, it may have no cash. When a company borrows money, the immediate result is to increase the cash balance. But no business would dream of treating the amount borrowed as a profit! It will have to be repaid in due course.

Cash flow and depreciation

The financial press often uses the term '**cash flow**' to mean 'retained profits plus depreciation' for a period. The point is that depreciation is merely an accounting entry in the period in which it appears as an expense. The only cash payment is for the purchase of a fixed asset at the start of its life. So since the accounts have deducted depreciation expense from turnover in measuring profit, it needs to

Table 3.3 Cash flow and depreciation (£'000)

	Original accounts	Depreciation up by 50%
Profit before depreciation	350	350
Depreciation expense	150	225
Profit before tax	200	125
Tax on profit (unchanged)	50	50
Profit after tax	150	75
Dividends payable	60	60
Retained profits	90	15
'Add back' depreciation	150	225
Internally generated cash flow	240	240

be 'added back' in order to convert the figure for profit into an estimate of 'cash flow' for the period. (Depreciation is not the only item in the profit and loss account which may not represent cash – see Table 3.2 – but it is often the single most important such item.)

If depreciation were literally a source of funds, it would be possible for a company to increase its cash balance merely by increasing its charge for depreciation expense in the profit and loss account. But doing this, of course, would then reduce reported profit to exactly the same extent! There would be no net effect on cash flow. (Changing the depreciation expense would not affect the tax bill, as the Inland Revenue have their own rules for 'writing-down allowances' (tax depreciation).)

Example
Suppose Hardstaff Engineering Limited increased its £150,000 depreciation expense in 1994 (see Table 1.4) by 50 per cent to £225,000. As Table 3.3 shows, the figure for 'cash flow' would remain unchanged.

Cash or profit: which matters more?

Both cash and profit matter, but people sometimes wonder whether one matters *more* than the other.

An entrepreneur who spots an opportunity to make a profit *ought* to be able to raise enough finance to invest in the project if capital markets are doing their job properly (see Chapter 7). On that view, profit matters more than cash. Someone who can identify (potential) profit can get cash to finance the project, and thus earn the profit. But someone who possesses cash will only get by way of yield the going risk-free rate of interest – and *no* profit.

Is it earnings per share or cash flow that drives share prices? Because earnings and cash often move together, it can be hard to interpret the evidence. But when there is a difference, which matters more? When American firms, some years ago, were allowed (for tax purposes) to switch from **FIFO** to **LIFO** stock valuation, the effect was to reduce both reported profits and tax payable (and thus to increase cash). The shares of companies which made the change on the whole performed better than the shares of companies which chose not to. The conclusion was that where earnings per share and cash flow did not move together, cash mattered more than profits.

What matters for shareholders' wealth is certainly not just the current year's reported earnings. A one-off accounting change with respect to stock valuation carries little if any message about the future. It should therefore not affect the share price much, except to the extent that there is an immediate (one-off) increase in cash due to a reduction in tax payable.

What matters more than the current year is expectations about future years – and this applies to cash flow as much as to earnings. It is misleading to suppose that the stock market attaches a constant price/earnings multiple to reported earnings per share. (If that were so, increasing reported earnings – even by means of some accounting 'trick' – would automatically increase the share price in the same proportion.)

That is not to say that accounting manipulations will never fool readers of accounts into mistaken estimates of the future. And if managers' remuneration partly depends on it, then managers at least are likely to care about reported earnings, even if shareholders do not.

Cash planning

Forecasting cash receipts from sales

A company's cash balance should be high enough to protect against any serious chance of running out, but not so high as to tie up excess funds in low-yielding uses. Financial managers of a business must decide what cash levels to aim at. Then they need to forecast the amount and timing of the likely future sources and uses of cash.

No company wants to run out of cash. It might be forced into **liquidation** by creditors it was unable to pay; or at least have to raise funds at a very high cost, and subject to burdensome conditions.

Careful forecasting of the amount and timing of future cash receipts and payments has the following benefits:

1. It tests the financial results of plans before making definite commitments.
2. It reveals possible future needs to raise more capital, which may take several months to arrange.
3. It avoids undesired accumulation of non-interest-bearing cash.

The most critical single estimate is very often the forecast of sales turnover. This nearly always represents a firm's main source of cash receipts. The forecast of cash receipts from sales is often subject to a large margin of error, since it depends on three different estimates, each of which may vary, as follows:

1. The physical volume of sales.
2. The average selling price per unit.
3. The average delay in payment (credit period taken).

Example
A financial manager is preparing a six-month cash forecast beginning in January. He decides to start by estimating cash receipts from sales, with the following basic assumptions:

- Sales revenue will be £200,000 a month for the first three months, rising to £250,000 for April and May, and to £300,000 in June.
- He expects 10 per cent in value of the sales to be for cash; the rest on credit terms resulting in the collection of cash on average one month after the date of the credit sale.
- At the beginning of the period debtors amount to £185,000.

Table 3.4 translates these assumptions into a schedule of expected cash receipts from sales, month by month. The value of goods sold

Table 3.4   Cash receipts from sales, January to June (£'000)

	January	February	March	April	May	June	Total
Underlying data							
Total sales	200	200	200	250	250	300	1,400
Credit sales (90%)	180	180	180	225	225	270	1,260
Cash receipts							
From debtors	185	180	180	180	225	225	1,175
Cash sales (10%)	20	20	20	25	25	30	140
Total	205	200	200	205	250	255	1,315

does not produce the same amount of cash in that period, due to credit. Over the whole six months, the various totals are as follows:

	£'000
Opening debtors	185
Add: Total sales	1,400
	1,585
Less: Closing debtors	270
Cash received in period	1,315

The £85,000 shortfall of cash received, as compared with total sales, is reflected in the £85,000 increase in debtors between the start and end of the period.

Forecasting other cash flows

Cash payments for operating expenses often relate fairly closely to sales volume. Purchases of materials normally vary with sales, though stock levels may fluctuate for a number of reasons (see Chapter 4).

Short-term sales fluctuations may affect other expenses less. The labour force, for example, may be stable in the short term. And one can predict some overhead expenses such as office rents. It may be more difficult to forecast certain discretionary expenses, such as research or staff training or advertising.

An overall cash forecast needs to include various other cash receipts and payments, even if there is no link with day-to-day operations. Receipts may come other than from sales: from disposing of old equipment; from issues of share capital or from borrowing; or from income on investments.

Payments other than for operating expenses may include: taxation; dividend payments; purchases of investments; acquiring fixed assets. Cash payments to acquire fixed assets will show up in operating expenses only as a result of charging depreciation expense (a non-cash item) over the asset's useful life.

Many of these forecasts – either their amounts or their timing – are not easy to make.

Pro forma balance sheets

The projected (pro forma) balance sheet method of forecasting funds requirements involves a forecast of *all* balance sheet items (not just cash) at a definite future date. It involves four major steps:

1. Forecasting the net total amount for each of the assets.
2. Listing the liabilities:
   (a) that will occur without special negotiation (such as trade creditors and **taxation**);
   (b) that have to be arranged (such as bank overdrafts).
3. Estimating profits for the period, less dividend payments. Since profit is a residual between two much larger amounts (sales turnover less total expenses), this may be subject to a wide margin of error.
4. Totalling the estimates of assets, liabilities and shareholders' funds, to reveal whether there remains a surplus or shortage of funds at the end of the period, to be invested or to be covered by raising more money.

The pro forma balance sheet method forecasts all the balance sheet items, not just cash. It can forecast certain financial ratios, such as return on net assets (or, indeed, it may be based on the assumption that certain financial ratios remain constant). It can also make rough – but often helpful – forecasts where forward plans may not yet exist in sufficient detail to allow cash flow forecasting.

The method forecasts balance sheet amounts only at the *end* of the period – not during the interim. It will therefore reveal maximum needs for funds only if the date shows the balance sheet at a time of maximum strain. (If there is doubt about the most suitable date to choose, make several projections at different dates.)

It is often worth noting *in writing* the key assumptions which underlie the forecasts; and it can be useful to try to assess the rough margin of error in the key items. It may also be worth preparing alternative forecasts using different assumptions. Modern data-processing equipment makes it easy to prepare detailed forecasts, and to test them by varying the assumptions ('sensitivity analysis').

Using the same assumptions, the projected balance sheet method and the detailed cash flow forecast approach should (of course) produce the same forecast for the end-of-period cash balance. The pro forma balance sheet method forces management to make explicit assumptions about fixed assets and working capital. These can be surprisingly easy to overlook in a cash flow forecast; yet they can be critical for many businesses.

4

Working capital

Working capital as a whole

The working capital cycle

Working capital is the excess of current assets over current liabilities. The two main items are **stocks** and **debtors**: they represent a firm's investment in goods which are unfinished, unsold, or unpaid for. Together these amount to nearly half the total assets of UK listed companies.

In view of its size, working capital is clearly important to many firms. (A useful ratio to calculate is working capital – defined as: stocks plus debtors plus a minimum level of cash, minus trade creditors and accruals – as a percentage of annual sales turnover.) A firm needs to determine a suitable level of investment in working capital – and then carry out the policy. (Managers may 'decide', for example, that debtors should average one month's credit sales; but someone still needs to make sure that the customers owe no more than that.)

Figure 4.1 shows the working capital cycle of a manufacturing business. The business first buys **raw materials** on credit, then uses labour and capital equipment (in various proportions in different industries) to convert the raw materials into **finished goods**. (Often there are intermediate stages of partly completed goods, known as **work-in-progress**.) On sale of the finished goods, legal title passes to the customer; and it is at this point that accounts recognize the

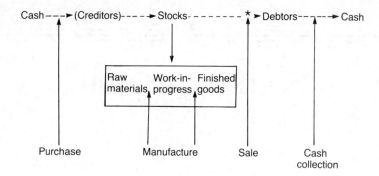

Figure 4.1   The working capital cycle

sale, and the profit thereon. The customer either pays cash or buys on credit. If the latter, when the debtor finally pays cash to settle his account he completes the transaction.

Thus the working capital cycle involves using cash to acquire raw materials to pay for overheads and to pay labour wages to convert materials over time into finished goods, which are then sold to customers and finally paid for. A profitable business should receive more cash at the end than it pays out during the working capital cycle. This is in order to pay (a) taxes on profits, (b) interest on borrowing, (c) dividends to shareholders, and (d) to replace capital assets.

In times of inflation, merely increasing the money amount of assets may not represent 'real' growth. This serious accounting problem affects both planning cash flows and measuring profit or loss. It is a worrying sign if a company can only maintain its existing level of business by raising more long-term capital. A healthy firm ought to be able at least to maintain its present real size out of 'internally generated' cash flow, though it may have to raise new long-term capital in order to finance real expansion.

Financing current assets

A hotel may always be full even though no single person is permanently resident. In the same way each item in working capital may be 'current' (since individual items of stock and debtors are continually turning into cash), but the net total may in effect represent a long-term investment requiring long-term finance to support it.

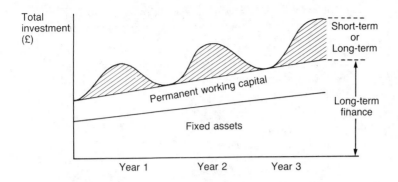

Figure 4.2 Financing seasonal current assets

Some companies' current asset needs may fluctuate during the year, perhaps because of seasonal sales or production patterns. Figure 4.2 shows two approaches to financing short-term peaks. A cautious company may aim to finance its maximum need by long-term funds. This will leave surplus cash to invest (at fairly low rates of return) during the off-peak period. A more aggressive company may finance only its minimum level with long-term funds. It will be in the riskier position of needing short-term finance during the seasonal peak. In either case the net total of 'working capital' may actually be fairly constant – since short-term 'surplus' cash or short-term borrowing (negative cash) would both themselves count as part of 'working capital'.

Liquidity

Accounting ratios based on aggregates need to be interpreted with caution. Table 4.1, for example, sets out Tesco's August 1993 working capital figures (slightly simplified and rounded). At first sight they may seem to be somewhat alarming. The **current ratio** is 0.35 and the **acid test ratio** only 0.11 (compared with 'rules of thumb' of 1.5 and 1.0 respectively). Thus current liabilities are more than double current assets, and net working capital is over £750 million negative! What is going on? Is Tesco going bankrupt, despite annual sales (excluding VAT) of £7,900 million?

In all financial and accounting work an essential rule to bear in mind is: don't panic! If a particular figure looks odd, it is worth spending a little time thinking why the number works out as it does.

Table 4.1   Tesco plc: working capital at 14 August 1993 (£m.)

Current assets:	
Stocks	283
Prepayments and other debtors	61
Cash and investments	73
	417
Current liabilities:	
Bank loans and overdrafts	70
Finance leases	25
Trade and other creditors and accruals	858
Corporation tax	174
Proposed interim dividend	48
	1,175

The £283 million stock (at cost) at 14 August 1993 (all available for sale in retail stores) represents less than two weeks' sales. So we could expect all of it to have turned into cash (at selling prices) by mid-September. Indeed Tesco's *stock* is a good deal more 'liquid' than most companies' debtors! Clearly the acid test ratio (which omits stock) gives much too gloomy a view for this type of retailer. In fact Tesco's sales in the month of September will probably yield over £600 million cash.

Not all the current liabilities are due for payment within the next month or so. The proposed interim dividend of £48 million will not be paid until late November. And about half of the £174 million corporation tax liability is also due at the end of November, nine months after the year end.

So even if we assumed that all other creditors (totalling £858 million) were due within the next month and a half, we could expect the company to have about £900 million cash available from one and a half month's sales. Thus Tesco's liquidity position seems adequate.

The truth is that a balance sheet gives only a rather crude idea of the real position; and we need to know a good deal about a particular business before we can begin to draw reliable conclusions. Accounting ratios are a very useful device to develop interesting questions – but they rarely provide all the answers.

Table 4.2 Stocks held in different industries

	BAT Industries (tobacco) %	British Aerospace (defence, motor vehicles, etc.) %	Guinness (wines and spirits) %	Tesco (food retailer) %
Raw materials and consumables	70	5	9	–
Stocks of maturing whisky and other spirits	–	–	79	–
Work in progress	} 25	} 119	} 1	–
Finished goods		} 22	} 11	–
Goods purchased for resale	} 5			100
(Progress payments)		(63)		
Development properties		17		
	100	100	100	100
Total stocks (£m.)	1,828	3,448	1,810	240
As percentage of total annual cost of sales	46	34	54	4
As percentage of total assets	38	32	22	5

Stocks

Types of stock

A manufacturing company holds three main types of stock (**inventory**): raw materials, work-in-progress, and finished goods. Table 4.2 shows the proportion of various types of stocks held by four different businesses. (The table also shows in each case total stocks related to annual cost of sales and to total assets.)

Most firms also hold stationery and maintenance supplies for use in the course of business. (They are usually included with raw materials stocks.)

Stocks are normally stated 'at cost' (or net realizable value if lower). The 'cost' of bringing a product to its present location and condition includes production overheads, based on the normal level of activity.

Levels of stock

Money invested in stocks ties up financial resources which could have been put to use elsewhere. This represents a real opportunity cost.

What determines stock levels? In general, the level of sales volume; the relationship between production and sales; the nature of the production process; and the cost of holding stocks. Service industries tend to have low stocks because they usually cannot 'store' their products in finished form. The same is true of some manufacturing companies, such as newspaper publishers or bakeries.

Raw materials stocks represent a buffer between outside suppliers and the demands of the manufacturing or assembly process. The level depends mainly on buying aspects: the nature of the goods (whether they are perishable, bulky, expensive); possible interruptions to supplies (for example, from strikes or crop failures); how quickly suppliers can deliver more goods (some Japanese car makers fly in supplies of components several times a day); the economics of bulk purchasing; and expected changes in future prices and in sales volume.

Work-in-progress depends largely on the method of production (such as batch versus flow); the importance of set-up costs; the length of the production process (bakeries will have lower work-in-progress than shipyards); and the possibility of subcontracting.

Finished goods stocks represent a buffer between customer demand and possibly intermittent supply from the purchasing or manufacturing side of the business. The level depends mainly on selling aspects: whether goods are being made to order; the reliability of sales forecasts; policy on the risk of stock-outs; and expected changes in sales volume.

Costs of holding stocks will vary for different industries, and may include handling, storage, insurance, and obsolescence, as well as interest on the money amount tied up. Average stockholding costs

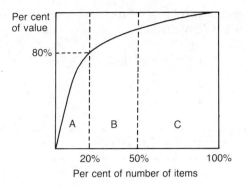

Figure 4.3 ABC analysis

may total as much as 25 per cent of book value a year. Hence there is a clear need to *balance* the benefits from holding stocks at any given time against the costs.

Managing stock

Forecasting whether a change in sales volume is temporary or more permanent can be crucial in deciding whether to change the rate of production. A wrong decision could mean either piling up unwanted stocks, or else running out of stock and thus losing potential sales. Either could be very expensive. The essence of business is judging the direction, extent and timing of changes in market conditions in the uncertain future.

In managing stocks, as in many other areas of management, a useful control device can be 'ABC analysis' (Figure 4.3). This employs the 'rule' that a small proportion (say, 20 per cent) of the total *number* of items will usually account for a large proportion (say, 80 per cent) of the total *value* of all items. (It is sometimes called the '80/20 rule'.) The implication is obvious: rather than pay equal attention to all items, it makes better commercial sense to look first at the few Class A items which account for most of the value, then at Class B items, and only at the end to consider the many small Class C items.

Another useful tool is to calculate the rate of **stock turnover** in a period, either in total or suitably analyzed. This is best done by dividing the cost of goods sold in a period by the amount of stock held. From a financial point of view, it is unfortunate that both production managers and marketing managers may have reasons for preferring high levels of stock (that is, low rates of stock turnover). In practice, therefore, it is important that managers be made responsible for *all* the costs of holding stock, including imputed interest.

Debtors

Individual customer credit

There are normally two decisions to make in advance about individual credit customers: whether to extend credit at all; and, if so, up to what maximum amount? There are several ways to check the creditworthiness of potential new customers: credit bureau reports, past financial statements, bank references, trade references from other suppliers, and perhaps even the views of the firm's own sales people.

Some customers ignore credit terms blatantly, either the total amount of credit or the period of credit taken. Ultimately there is an implied threat of legal action against customers who do not pay amounts due according to the credit terms agreed. But it is better to avoid this if possible: the supplier wants his money, but dislikes the trouble and expense of taking formal legal action against debtors.

In the end, however, a seller may prefer not to do business with a customer who takes too long to pay. Recently one of the UK's biggest book publishers closed the credit account of a large book retailer 'because of persistent late payments over an extended period'. Publishers need retail outlets for their books; but the outlets also need suppliers.

The credit control system should include a regular review of all customers, to ensure that they are not exceeding their maximum credit limits (either in amount or in time). But people will tend to ignore unduly low credit limits. One useful way to get money from debtors can be simply to *telephone* and ask directly why they haven't paid! Some companies even telephone customers *during* the credit period to confirm that they can expect to receive the amount involved on the due date. This also enables them to sort out any queries in good time. Such behaviour is not 'unsporting'; it is merely businesslike.

Overall credit control

A powerful tool for measuring debtors is to calculate the average number of **days' sales** still owing at the end of a period.

Example
Sales for the past calendar year amounted to £180,000, and debtors at the end of December totalled £30,000. So (ignoring VAT for the moment), 61 days' sales were outstanding:

$$\frac{£30,000}{£180,000} \times 365 = 61 \text{ days}$$

Or we could do the sum in two stages:

Daily sales $\quad \dfrac{£180,000}{365} = £493$

Outstanding $\quad \dfrac{£30,000}{£493} = 61 \text{ days}$

If December sales were £25,000 and November sales £15,000, a more accurate estimate, relating to sales month by month, could suggest an average credit period of 41 days. We assume that customers pay in date order. Then total end-December debtors of £30,000 include all of December's £25,000 sales (= 31 days) plus £5,000 of November's £15,000 sales (= 10 days).

Unfortunately value added tax (VAT) complicates the position, as sales exclude VAT while debtors include it. Assuming all credit sales are subject to VAT at 17½ per cent, debtors *excluding* VAT are only

$$£30,000 \times \frac{100}{100 + 17.5} = £25,532$$

Hence the actual number of days' sales outstanding in debtors is:

$$\frac{£25,532}{£180,000} \times 365 = 51.8 \text{ days}$$

The alternative calculation would result in 32.1 days: December's

£25,000 (ex VAT) sales = 31 days, plus £532 out of November's £15,000 sales = 1.1 days.

The amount invested in debtors (**accounts receivable**) depends partly on the volume of credit sales. Since most firms want to increase sales volume, the main way of trying to control total credit outstanding is to limit the average *period* of credit taken by customers. This depends both on the credit terms offered, and on the effectiveness of the seller's collection procedures. The gain from good credit control can be very large.

Example

Over four years, one major company reduced its average credit period from 137 days to 92 days. With sales of £500 million a month, the saving of 45 days' credit amounted to saving an investment in debtors of £750 million! At the then interest rate of 14 per cent a year, the interest saved exceeded £100 million a year. Such a prize would certainly make the employment of a few competent credit controllers very worthwhile.

Good credit managers are quick to respond to changes in the overall pattern of debtors: they also tend to operate with specific targets, either in absolute money amounts or (preferably) in terms of average days' sales outstanding.

If the average credit period which customers are taking is too high, or increasing beyond target, management should find out why. Has **trade credit** policy changed? Or the mix of customers? Is the company giving suitable priority to the largest customers? Sending out invoices and statements promptly? Chasing up slow payers vigorously enough?

Risk and return from debtors

Selling for cash avoids any need to 'invest' in debtors by (in effect) lending them money. But most companies want to offer credit terms at least nearly as attractive as their competitors. The two main risks in extending trade credit are that the customer will either take too long to pay, or else fail to pay at all (bad debts).

In practice opportunity losses due to debtors taking too long to pay tend to be far more important (though easy to overlook) than losses – sometimes dramatic – due to **bad debts**. For example, some government departments or large companies are very bad debtors, even though their accounts may be most unlikely to end up as 'bad debts'. Being 'important' customers, they often take much longer to pay than the official credit terms offered. Yet nobody doubts that they will pay all right *in the end*. In that sense they are 'good' debts, but often very slow. Time is money . . . The big company which succeeded in reducing by 1½ months the average credit period taken by its customers is notorious for taking a very long time to pay its own bills! (Hence the Latin tag: 'Bis dat qui cito dat' – 'He gives twice who gives quickly'.)

One way of viewing the opportunity cost of credit is to recognize the true cost of offering a **cash discount** to customers who pay promptly. If customers on average take 45 days after invoice date before paying, then a 2 per cent discount for payment of cash within 10 days would cost 2 per cent for 35 days credit saved. This works out to be an *annual* rate of over 20 per cent a year ($2 \times 365/35 = 20.9$ per cent a year). What matters here is the 45 days' credit *actually* being taken, not the company's official credit terms of (say) 30 days.

There are two problems in practice with offering cash discounts for early payment. First, debtors who cannot pay soon enough to claim the cash discount may think they are then entitled to pay very late. Second, it can be tricky withdrawing the cash discount at a later date if the firm wants to change the policy. Another possible approach would be to *charge* interest on overdue accounts, but this is not popular nor easy to implement (though the threat of it may hurry up some debtors).

The 'return' from extending credit to customers consists of the marginal **contribution** to profit from the extra sales made (assuming that there would have been no sale without offering credit). Trade credit policy has to balance the possible return against the risk. Incurring *no* bad debts at all suggests that a firm is probably taking too few credit risks. In view of the likely returns forgone, it makes little sense to refrain from making sales on credit to 99 customers on the off-chance that the 100th may fail to pay the whole amount due. In this respect commercial companies, normally having much larger contribution margins, can well afford to take larger credit risks than can banks.

Factors enable firms to reduce working capital tied up in debtors. The factoring company buys some or all of a firm's debts, at full value less a factoring charge, and then undertakes to collect them. Sometimes any bad debts remain to be borne by the firm itself, not by the factor (which affects the charges). The service may also include sales ledger administration.

Spontaneous creditors

The amount of current liabilities to deduct from current assets determines the extent to which working capital needs long-term funds to finance it. Some current liabilities need little special arrangement, such as trade **creditors**, accrued charges and tax. They occur more or less spontaneously; and we discuss them below. Other items of short-term finance, such as bank overdrafts and short-term loans, normally carry interest and do have to be negotiated. They are better regarded as part of corporate borrowing ('debt'), and we discuss them in Chapter 7.

Trade creditors

Suppliers often sell goods and services on credit rather than for cash, with a time lag of up to three months between supply and payment. Unlike bank overdrafts, trade credit does not need much formal negotiation; yet for many firms it can be an important 'permanent' source of finance.

Purchasers should be aware of any cash discounts which suppliers are offering for prompt payment. The implied annual rate of interest can be high, so if financial resources permit, it is often worthwhile taking advantage of them.

At the other end of the payment scale, it may seem almost cost-free to take extended credit from suppliers. But the obvious risk is that the supply of goods or services may eventually be stopped, possibly at a most inconvenient time. Also if supplies are ever short, better payers may well receive preference.

The average period of credit to customers is often similar to that which suppliers allow. But the total amount of debtors may often be larger than total trade creditors ('**accounts payable**'). The difference comes from the profit margin, and also from certain cash expenses, such as wages. Firms with high added value will tend to have low trade creditors, since much of their costs will consist of wages rather than raw materials or bought-in parts.

Some other non-cash expenses, such as depreciation, will not be reflected in trade creditors; but trade creditors may include amounts outstanding for fixed assets purchased. Indeed, separate disclosure seems a good idea. For example, Thames Water plc discloses: trade creditors – operating £66.5 million; capital £117.5 million.

Accrued charges consist of costs incurred for goods and services which suppliers have not yet invoiced. Examples would be utility charges, rent and business rates, or audit fees. Amounts owing for social security and other taxes include VAT and PAYE and social security tax deducted from employees' wages.

Tax on profits

Corporation tax payable on profits appears under a separate heading both in the profit and loss account and in the balance sheet. It includes UK corporation tax on UK profits, and foreign taxes payable on profits earned overseas. Tax on the current year's profits (other than deferred tax: see Chapter 7) is normally payable within less than twelve months, and therefore appears as a current liability.

There are special rules for computing tax on profits, so 'taxable profit' is not the same as reported profit before tax in the accounts. In particular, Inland Revenue **capital allowances** (writing down allowances) replace the depreciation expense in the accounts. Thus a UK company cannot reduce its tax bill by increasing its book depreciation charge. Moreover the tax rules may completely disallow certain legal, entertaining and other expenses; or there may be timing differences both for revenues and for expenses.

Dividends payable

Most UK companies pay an 'interim' dividend on ordinary shares during the financial year, and propose a 'final' dividend to be paid after the year end. The balance sheet shows the proposed final dividend as a current liability, on the assumption that shareholders will approve it at the annual general meeting. The profit and loss account shows the total of interim and final dividends as an appropriation of profit (not as a charge against it, since dividends are not an expense).

In some countries the practice is to include ordinary dividends only when they have actually been declared, and thus become a legal liability. In such cases the balance sheet will normally show no current liability for any unpaid final dividend, but larger retained profits in shareholders' funds.

Accounts show dividends net of **advance corporation tax (ACT)** both in the profit and loss account and in the balance sheet. Where ACT is irrecoverable (because of losses or overseas earnings), any extra amount is shown as part of corporation tax, not as part of dividends.

Income received in advance

Some kinds of enterprise, for example magazine publishers or schools, tend to receive income in advance of providing services. Any such amounts not yet fully earned by the end of a financial year appear under a separate heading. Strictly the current 'liability' is to provide the service in future, not to pay money. But if, for some reason, the service were never provided, there would probably be a legal liability to repay at least a proportion of the money received in advance. (The opposite is prepayments, where a firm pays in advance for certain services, such as rent or insurance. These are normally included with debtors.)

.

5

Basic capital project appraisal

Background

The capital investment process

Capital investment means spending money now in the hope of getting more back later. 'Investment' as such is not worthwhile: it needs to yield a *profit*. There are several key steps in the investment process (see Table 5.1). Probably the most important step is the first – generating worthwhile ideas for capital investments. They may stem from spotting opportunities or from responding to problems in all areas of the business. Then one needs to gather information – about competitors, customers, technology, and so on. There may be many different ways to achieve the aim of a project. Most companies try to screen some out before spending too much time on them.

Capital investment projects may often encompass the whole range of business: finance, marketing, production, R&D, strategy. Hence large projects involve groups of people from many parts of the business. There will be a need for detailed engineering estimates, market forecasts and so on.

Later parts of this chapter and the next deal in detail with the *financial* aspects of capital projects. But often the 'non-financial' aspects are more important. Even after the final decision to commit funds to a project, it still remains to implement the decision. This vital process may take many months, and mistakes here can be very costly. Where conditions have changed, the actual project may not

Table 5.1 Key steps in the capital investment process

1. Generate ideas – opportunities and solutions to problems.
2. Search out relevant information.
3. Identify possible alternatives.
4. Determine specific project details.
5. Evaluate financial consequences.
6. Assess 'non-financial' consequences.
7. Make a decision . . . . If to proceed,
8. Implement and control project.
9. Monitor results.

be quite the same as the one management approved. Post-project audits are discussed in Chapter 6.

Estimating net benefits

It can be hard to estimate a project's future net benefits. What consumers will want in a few years' time, what competitors will be up to, how production methods and technology may change – all are uncertain. Yet they may affect the project's life, sales volume, selling prices, costs. And even in so-called market economies, firms have to cope with extensive and continually changing government interference.

Three main kinds of capital project are: replacing equipment, to reduce costs or improve quality; expanding productive capacity, to meet growing demand; or providing new facilities to make new products. An expansion or new-product project may promise to increase sales revenue by more than operating costs. A cost reduction project, in contrast, may not affect sales revenue at all: the net benefit of the project is lower future operating costs than would otherwise occur (see Figure 5.1).

In estimating how much net improvement will result from a project, the forecast of sales revenue is often critical. For example, publishers may be able to calculate production costs quite closely, with a fixed selling price, but sales volume may be very uncertain; or petrol companies may be fairly sure how much petrol they will sell, but not what the selling prices will be. On the other hand, shipbuilding on a fixed-price contract would provide certain sales revenue, but uncertain costs and timing. Reaching a sensible answer may depend on asking the right questions. For example, for a capital project the choices may be:

1. *Whether or not* to buy machine H.
2. Whether to buy *machine H or machine J*.
3. Whether to buy machine H *now or later*.
4. *How many* machine Hs to buy.

We shall not be concerned in this chapter with how to *finance* capital projects. As a rule it is best to separate the question whether a project is worthwhile from the (usually less important) question of how to finance it. Often companies, in effect, have a pool of funds from which they can finance *all* worthwhile projects (see Chapter 7).

Simple appraisal methods

Average accounting return on investment

Profitability is often expressed as an annual rate of return on investment (ROI).

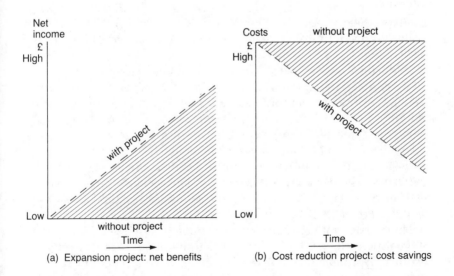

(a) Expansion project: net benefits   (b) Cost reduction project: cost savings

Figure 5.1 Incremental benefits for different kinds of project

Table 5.2   Project A versus Project B

		Project A £'000		Project B £'000	
Investment outflow	Year 0		−9		−15
Cash receipts	Year 1	+3		+7	
	Year 2	+4		+8	
	Year 3	+8		+9	
		———		———	
			+15		+24
			———		———
Net profit (3 years)			+6		+9
Average annual profit			+2		+3
$\dfrac{\text{Average annual profit}}{\text{Initial investment}} = \text{ROI}$		$\dfrac{2}{9} = 22\%$		$\dfrac{3}{15} = 20\%$	

Example 1

Table 5.2 shows two rival capital projects, each lasting for three years. Project A requires an initial investment of £9,000, Project B of £15,000. Project A will produce cash receipts of £3,000 in Year 1, £4,000 in Year 2, and £8,000 in Year 3; while Project B will produce cash receipts of £7,000 in Year 1, £8,000 in Year 2, and £9,000 in Year 3.

Deducting each project's initial investment from its total cash receipts gives the overall net profit (return). When we deduct the initial investment from total cash receipts (in effect charging 'depreciation'), Project B yields a larger *total profit* (9 versus 6). The projects have the same life (three years), so Project B also yields a larger *average annual profit* than Project A (3 versus 2). But if we divide the average annual profit by the initial amount invested, Project A produces a higher annual *rate of return on investment* than Project B (22 per cent versus 20 per cent); and using this method, we would say that Project A is better.

The average rate of return on investment (normally in terms of an annual percentage) does tell us something about a capital project's estimated profitability. But the averaging process cuts out relevant information about the *timing* of the returns. Also an extra £2,000 cash inflow in Year 4 would reduce Project B's average rate of return to 18.3 per cent (= 2.75/15), being now averaged over four years, not three. (Project A's rate of return would remain unchanged at 22.2 per cent.)

Example 2

Suppose we now compare Project A (as before) with a new Project C. Project A's profits (NB: not its cash inflows) are £1,000, £2,000, and £6,000 in Years 1, 2, and 3; while Project C's profits, let us suppose, are £6,000, £2,000, and £1,000 (in the reverse order to Project A).

The average rate of return on investment is the same for both projects: 22 per cent per year (£2,000/£9,000). The only difference is that Project C gives a profit (and cash inflow) £5,000 larger than Project A in Year 1, but £5,000 smaller in Year 3. In total, over the whole life of the projects, this difference balances out; but the larger cash inflow in Year 1 under Project C can be invested for two years to yield a positive *extra* return. Allowing for this, Project C is better than Project A. But this relevant fact is not revealed by the average rate of return which ignores the timing of the returns.

Where the returns happen to be the same in each year of a project's life, this timing objection matters less. But the use of average accounting return on investment also raises some tricky questions of definition. For example: What do we mean by 'return' and by 'investment'? How do we handle tax and inflation? How do we estimate the life of the project? How can we determine the minimum acceptable rate of return?

Payback

Even more widely used than 'rate of return on investment' is the **payback** method. This shows how many years it will take before a capital project 'pays back' the amount invested (that is, before the cumulative cash receipts exceed the initial investment). The shorter the payback period, the better. To calculate the payback period we look at after-tax cash receipts from a project, rather than accounting profits. Thus we only deduct cash expenses from sales receipts, not depreciation.

Example 1

Let us now look again at Project A and Project C, each costing £9,000, assuming that they generate cash evenly throughout each

Table 5.3   Cash flows for Project A and Project C.

		Project A £'000	Project C £'000
Initial investment	Year 0	−9	−9
Cash receipts	Year 1	+3	+8
	Year 2	+4	+4
	Year 3	+8	+3

year (see Table 5.3). The payback period for Project A is easy to calculate. £3,000 is repaid in Year 1, £4,000 in Year 2, and £8,000 in Year 3. Thus Project A's payback period is 2¼ years (two years totalling £7,000, plus one-quarter of a year at £8,000 equals the initial investment of £9,000). In a similar way we can calculate Project C's payback period as being only 1¼ years. Figure 5.2 shows a graphical picture of the payback periods.

The payback method of project appraisal has one clear advantage over the average rate of return on investment method: it takes timing into account, at least to some extent. It is also simple to calculate and easy to understand, which may explain why so many companies use it. But the payback method ignores cash receipts *after*

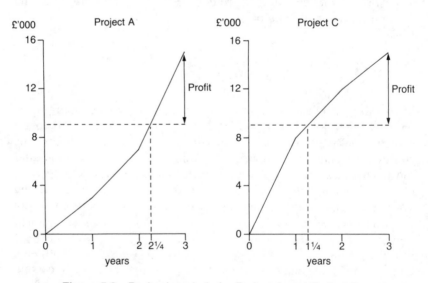

Figure 5.2   Payback periods for Project A and Project C

payback. This is vital: there can be no profit unless we get back *more* than the original investment.

Example 2
Suppose that in Year 4 Project A produces a cash inflow of £20,000 while Project C produces only £1,000. According to the payback method, that would *not* change the relative merits of the two projects: Project C would still be 'better' than Project A because of its shorter payback period. This clearly does not make business sense!

While it may be a useful relative measure of risk (faster payback means less risk), the payback method does not measure profit. Nor is it clear how to determine a suitable minimum payback period criterion. After all, some very successful drugs have taken more than ten years to pay back all the investment in research and development. In practice, companies often use payback as a rough screening device. And where the returns happen to be the *same* in each year, then the payback method may *rank* projects in the same order as more accurate methods of assessing whether capital projects will yield a profit – to which we now turn.

Measuring profit over time

The 'time value' of money

Capital investment involves spending money now in the hope of larger returns later. To tell whether the returns are large enough, we need a way to compare returns in the future with investment now – to compare money amounts over time.

A given amount of money now is worth more than the same amount of money in future. Why? Because it can be invested today to yield a return in the meantime.

Interest rates do not merely reflect inflation: they also allow for time preference and risk (see Chapter 2). Some types of financial **investment** (in the stock market) are more risky than others (bank deposits). They require a higher return to compensate for the higher risk.

Let us suppose that we can invest money today to yield 12 per

Table 5.4 Future values of '£1,000 now' at 12 per cent a year

	End of Year 0 (now) £	End of Year 1 £	End of Year 2 £	End of Year 3 £
Future values	1,000 →	1,120 →	1,254 →	1,405
Present values	1,000 ←————— 1,120 1,000 ←————————————— 1,254 1,000 ←————————————————————— 1,405			

cent a year. Then £1,000 invested today will accumulate (compounding annually) to the following amounts:

In 1 year's time, to £1,000 × 1.12   = £1,000 × 1.120 = £1,120

In 2 years' time, to £1,000 × $(1.12)^2$ = £1,000 × 1.254 = £1,254

In 3 years' time, to £1,000 × $(1.12)^3$ = £1,000 × 1.405 = £1,405

Thus, using an interest rate of 12 per cent a year, the future value of '£1,000 now' is £1,405 at the end of three years. Or, looking at it the other way round: the **present value** of '£1,405 to be received at the end of three years' is £1,000 now (see Table 5.4).

What, then, is the present value of '£1,000 to be received at the end of three years'? Clearly it must be £712, as follows:

$$\frac{£1,000}{(1.12)^3} = \frac{£1,000}{1.405} = £712$$

We can prove this by showing what would happen if we invested £712 at 12 per cent a year. Each year the effect of compound interest is to add 12 per cent of the start-of-year cumulative amount invested, as follows:

After 1 year the amount becomes: £712 + £85 = £797

After 2 years the amount becomes: £797 + £96 = £893

After 3 years the amount becomes: £893 + £107 = £1,000

Thus we can see the present value of £1,000 to be received at any future date (see Table 5.5).

Table 5.5 Present values of '£1,000 in future' at 12 per cent a year

	End of Year 0 (now) £	End of Year 1 £	End of Year 2 £	End of Year 3 £
Future values	712 →	797 →	893 →	1,000
Present values	893 ←————— 1,000 797 ←——————————— 1,000 712 ←————————————————— 1,000			

Assuming an interest rate of 12 per cent a year, the present value of any amount (call it 'a') to be received at the end of three years is $0.712a$. Thus 0.712 is the **discount factor** for three years at 12 per cent a year. It is equivalent to $1/(1.12)^3$. (We shall normally use discount factors correct to three decimal places. This is quite accurate enough for most practical purposes.)

In effect, this gives us an 'exchange rate over time'. Just as compound factors tell us the future values of present-day money amounts, so discount factors tell us the present value of future money amounts. (See Appendix B for table of discount factors.)

Net terminal value

We have been assuming that we can always invest any sum of money now to yield an annual return of 12 per cent. In practice it is not always easy to estimate this rate of interest (the opportunity cost of capital). As we saw in Chapter 2, the make-up of an 'interest rate' can be quite complex.

If money costs 12 per cent a year, then that is the minimum **required rate of return** on a capital investment project (sometimes called the 'hurdle rate'). Why invest in a capital project expected to yield *less* than 12 per cent a year? We need to get a higher return from capital projects for the investment to be worthwhile. (At this stage we ignore possible differences in riskiness.)

Example
Nellam Ltd is thinking of expanding its fleet of vehicles by one 20-ton truck costing £26,000. It would operate for four years and then be scrapped, so the **straight-line depreciation** charge would be £6,500 a year. The company expects net cash flows from the extra

business to be £6,000, £7,000, £9,000, and £11,000 in Years 1 to 4. Should Nellam acquire the extra truck?

We can compare the two options, as follows:

1. Invest £26,000 in buying the truck, and receive the cash flows resulting.
2. Do not buy the truck – in which case Nellam will merely earn the going interest rate of 12 per cent a year on the £26,000.

Table 5.6 sets out the financial results. Since we are looking at a project with a four-year life, we need to allow for Nellam to reinvest any cash received before the end of Year 4. Then we can compare the two options as at the end of Year 4. We assume Nellam can invest cash to earn the going interest rate of 12 per cent a year. Thus, for instance, Nellam can invest the £9,000 cash received at the end of Year 3 to earn 12 per cent interest in Year 4, becoming £10,800 by the end of Year 4. Similarly for other cash receipts in earlier years.

Clearly the investment in the truck is not worthwhile. Its net terminal value is negative (−£2,621). Rather than buying the truck (which provides only £38,290 by the end of Year 4) Nellam would be better off earning 12 per cent a year on the £26,000 for four years (to accumulate to £40,911 by the end of Year 4).

The **net terminal value** (**NTV**) method compounds a project's cash inflows to the terminal (horizon) date, using the hurdle rate (or 'required rate of return'). It then compares the cumulative amount at

Table 5.6   Net terminal value for Nellam's new truck project

End of year	Cash flow (£)	Compound factor	Amount at end of Year 4 (£)
Do not buy truck			
0 (now)	−£26,000 × (1.12)^4	1.5735	−40,911
Invest in truck			
1	+6,000 × (1.12)^3	1.4049 = 8,429 ⎤	
2	+7,000 × (1.12)^2	1.2544 = 8,781 ⎥ +38,290	
3	+9,000 × (1.12)^1	1.1200 = 10,080 ⎥	
4	+11,000 × (1.12)^0	1.0000 = 11,000 ⎦	
Net terminal value			−2,621

the horizon date with the result from simply investing the initial amount at that rate for the project's life.

A variant, called the **compounding to horizon (CH)** method, determines *what is* the compound rate of interest needed on the initial investment to produce the same cash amount as the project itself will produce by the horizon date. In Nellam's case, an annual rate of 10.2 per cent will compound £26,000 to £38,290 by the end of Year 4. Since this is less than the going interest rate of 12.0 per cent, the truck project is not good enough.

Discounted cash flow methods

Net present value

The **net present value (NPV)** method of investment appraisal (like the net terminal value method: see above) calculates a project's profit by comparing cash payments and cash receipts at the same point in time. Rather than looking at the end of a project's life, however, it looks at the start. It does so by *discounting* expected future cash flows back to the present (that is, back to the 'end of Year 0'). It then compares the total 'present value' of the future cash receipts with the initial capital investment in the project.

The NPV method multiplies future cash flows by a suitable discounting factor. (This is the same as dividing by the appropriate compounding factor.) The discounting factor depends on two things: the **discount rate** (or interest rate); and how far ahead in time the cash flow arises.

Example
Looking again at the Nellam truck project, we see that its net present value (as set out in Table 5.7) is negative. Hence the project is not worthwhile. The cost of investing in the project is £26,000 now, while the present value of the expected future cash receipts (discounted at 12 per cent a year) is only £24,334. That is hardly smart business: it represents a loss (in present value terms) of £1,666.

The principles used to calculate net present value are exactly the same as for net terminal value. Hence both methods always give the same signal about whether or not a project is worthwhile. The only

Table 5.7 Net present value for Nellam's new truck project

End of year	Cash flow (£)		Discount factor at 12% a year		Present value (£)
0 (now)	−26,000		1.0000		−26,000
1	+6,000	×	0.8929	= +5,357	⎫
2	+7,000	×	0.7972	= +5,580	⎪ +24,334
3	+9,000	×	0.7118	= +6,406	⎬
4	+11,000	×	0.6355	= +6,991	⎭
Net present value					−1,666

difference is that NPV compares amounts at the start of the project, NTV at the end.

The numbers from the Nellam truck project show that NPV is exactly equivalent to NTV:

NPV (EOY 0): −£1,666 × 1.5735 = NTV (EOY 4): −£2,621

or

NTV (EOY 4): −£2,621 × 0.6355 = NPV (EOY 0): −£1,666.

In computing net present value (and net terminal value), we have assumed that cash flows arise only at year ends. In practice they may occur evenly throughout the year, but our assumption is often more convenient and is unlikely to change the decision. Remember that nearly all the numbers we use are only estimates.

Note that we round all amounts to the nearest pound. There is no advantage in spurious accuracy. Figures for cash flows are usually no more than estimates; and the discount rate used is nearly always only approximate. (The only reason why, unusually, we used discount factors to *four* decimal places – rather than three – was to avoid minor 'rounding errors' when showing that NPV and NTV methods were precisely equivalent.)

In practice firms use net present value rather than net terminal value. Managers prefer to think in terms of present values rather than in terms of future values. Also NPV enables them to compare different projects as at the same point in time (EOY 0); whereas projects with different lives would have different terminal dates, which would make it hard to compare NTVs directly.

The great advantage of the net terminal value method, at least in a textbook, is to clarify the precise meaning of the interest rate used in

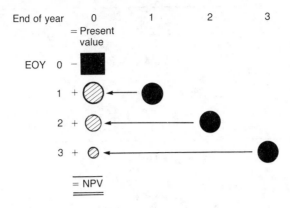

Figure 5.3 The discounting process in net present value (NPV)

discounted cash flow methods. The compounding approach of the NTV method makes quite explicit the **'opportunity cost'** nature of the interest rate.

The NPV method, as we have seen, compares cash receipts and payments expected to result from a capital project. It multiplies them by discounting factors to translate all expected future cash flows from a project into 'present values' (that is, into end-of-Year 0 money terms). Figure 5.3 shows this approach graphically.

Discounted cash flow (DCF) methods involve forecasting both the amount and the timing of **incremental cash flows** which will occur if a particular project is undertaken, but not otherwise. Note that DCF methods deal with cash flows and *not* with accounting profits, income and expenses. Hence in estimating future cash flows we ignore non-cash expenses such as depreciation. To tell whether a project is expected to be profitable, we simply see whether or not the present value of the project's discounted net receipts exceeds the present value of the cash investment.

In other words, we first *value* the project, and then compare that amount with the project's cost. This may simply be the initial amount of the cash investment; but sometimes projects consist of several cash payments spread out over time, which themselves need to be discounted back to present value terms.

If the project's value is more than its cost it will have a positive net present value after deducting the cost from the total present value. It is then worth undertaking on financial grounds: it will increase the owner's wealth. Figure 5.4 shows a way to picture this valuation process.

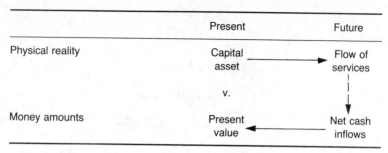

Figure 5.4   Valuing a capital asset

The NPV method, in theory, will always give the correct answer, if one assumes all three of the following:

1. The amounts and timing of all the cash flows are correctly forecast.
2. The opportunity cost of capital is correctly estimated.
3. There are no relevant non-financial aspects to a capital project.

The sweeping and unrealistic nature of these three necessary qualifications makes it clear that in practice no method of analysis can guarantee to give a precisely 'correct' answer. The business world is too uncertain for that.

Variants on net present value

Companies sometimes may choose to 'ration' capital, for strategic or other reasons. A variant of the net present value method may then be useful, called the **profitability index (PI)**. This method divides the present value of a project's cash inflows by the present value of the investment. In the Nellam truck project this is £24,334/ £26,000 = 0.94. Clearly if the profitability index exceeds 1.00, the signal from the numbers is 'go ahead' – just like a positive net present value. (Sometimes the index is multiplied by 100, which would give a figure of 94 in the Nellam truck project.)

Where capital is 'rationed' (see Chapter 6), companies may use the profitability index to rank projects. Where not all projects with a positive net present value can go ahead, a company may prefer those with the higher PIs (rather than those with the higher absolute NPVs). One problem with PIs may be how to interpret the meaning of the discount rate, if it does *not* represent the opportunity cost of capital.

Another use for the profitability index may be to indicate the margin of safety for a project. If, for example, the PI is above 1.00 but not more than (say) 1.20, then the estimates of future cash flows don't have to be much out before the PI may fall below 1.00. On the other hand, where the PI exceeds 1.50, there is quite a large margin of error before the project fails to be worthwhile.

The NPV method 'capitalizes' future cash inflows, and compares their discounted total with the initial investment. Where cash inflows are the same each year, it may sometimes be easier to 'annualize' the initial investment, and compare that with the (equal) annual cash inflows. (A similar approach can help to compare projects with different lives.)

Suppose the Nellam truck project were going to produce equal annual cash inflows each year. The **annualized cost** of the £26,000 initial investment (at 12 per cent over four years) is £26,000/3.037 = £8,561. Hence the project would be acceptable only if the annual cash inflows exceeded £8,561. (3.037 = 0.893 + 0.797 + 0.712 + 0.635, the discount factors for Years 1–4 at 12 per cent.)

Internal rate of return

Another method of discounting cash flows is the **internal rate of return (IRR)** method (also called the DCF yield method).

The net present value method lists the amount and timing of all the expected future cash flows from a project; and the internal rate of return method does the same. The NPV method then applies a preselected (**criterion**) discount rate to see whether the net total of all the discounted cash flows is positive or negative. If the NPV is positive, then the project is worthwhile (from a financial point of view); if the NPV is negative, it is not.

In contrast, the IRR method determines, by trial and error, *what is* the (initially unknown) discount rate which, when applied to the same cash flows, will produce a net present value of exactly zero. That discount rate is the project's 'internal rate of return'. To see whether or not a project is worthwhile, the firm must compare its IRR with the criterion rate.

Example

In Table 5.7, using a 12 per cent discount rate, we found an NPV of −£1,666 for Nellam's new truck project. The project's IRR must

Table 5.8 Calculating IRR by trial and error

End of year	Cash flow (£)	Discount factor @ 8%	Discount factor @ 10%	Present value (£) @ 8%	Present value (£) @ 10%
0 (now)	−26,000	1.000	1.000	−26,000	−26,000
1	+6,000	0.926	0.909	+5,556	+5,454
2	+7,000	0.857	0.826	+5,999	+5,782
3	+9,000	0.794	0.751	+7,146	+6,759
4	+11,000	0.735	0.683	+8,085	+7,513
Net present value				+786	−492

therefore be less than 12 per cent, since we need to discount the project's future cash inflows rather less. If we recalculate the NPV using both a 10 per cent discount rate and an 8 per cent discount rate (see Table 5.8), we can see that the project's IRR lies between 8 per cent and 10 per cent, a little closer to 10 per cent. We can estimate the IRR by interpolation, as follows:

$$IRR = 10\% - \frac{492}{492 + 786} \times 2\%$$

$$= 10\% - \frac{492 \times 2}{1278}$$

$$= 10\% - 0.76\% = 9.24\%$$

Nellam would need to compare the IRR of 9.2 per cent with the required minimum hurdle rate in order to tell whether 9.2 per cent is an acceptable rate of return. If the required rate is 12 per cent, clearly it is not acceptable. Figure 5.5 shows what the truck project's net present value amounts to for a whole range of discount rates. Three values in particular are worth noting:

A. Using a 0 per cent discount rate, the NPV is +£7,000.

B. The net present value is zero at a discount rate of 9.2 per cent. This is the internal rate of return.

C. Using a 12 per cent discount rate (the hurdle rate), the NPV is −£1,666.

A project with a higher internal rate of return may not always be 'better' than a project with a lower IRR, even on financial grounds.

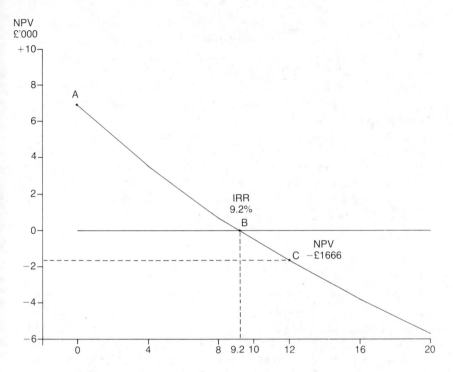

Figure 5.5   NPV of Nellam's truck project at various discount rates

This is for two main reasons. First, the amount invested may be different. Is a 40 per cent IRR better than 25 per cent? Perhaps not, if the 40 per cent is earned on an investment of £100, the 25 per cent on an investment of £10,000. The second reason is that IRR, in effect, assumes **reinvestment** (of cash inflows) at the project's own internal rate of return. But this is unlikely to be the actual opportunity cost of capital; which makes it hard to compare two different projects, especially if they have different lives.

The IRR method is also subject to certain other technical problems: for example, if there are negative cash flows during the project's life. And it is not so versatile as the NPV method in some respects: for example, NPV can use different discount rates for different kinds of cash flows, or for different periods, which IRR cannot.

Even where one of the DCF methods appears to show that a project is worthwhile, it is still important for managers to satisfy themselves about the business case for it. In other words, *why* should a particular project make a profit? If there seems to be no specific reason, then the apparent result of the financial assessment must be open to doubt. All experienced managers know how easy it is for optimistic assumptions to make a project look good!

It cannot be stressed too strongly that financial estimates are nearly always just that – estimates. Often with a very large margin of error. In addition to the DCF calculations, strategic factors such as competitors' actions may need to be considered. The final decision for marginal capital investment proposals often depends on the ability of their proposers to sell the idea. A good track record from previous capital investments may also carry weight at the final decision stage. Judgement about the uncertain business future is likely to be far more important than technical proficiency with DCF.

Discounted payback

The payback method (discussed above) can also use discounted cash flows, to give a 'discounted payback' period. Table 5.9 shows the result of discounting Project A's cash inflows of £3,000, £4,000, and £8,000 in Years 1, 2, and 3, at 12 per cent a year.

Thus the positive net present value would be +£2,653, and the *discounted* payback period would be 2.55 years. (This is £5,867 pv received by the end of Year 2 – assuming cash received evenly throughout the year *for this purpose* – plus 3,133/5,696 = 0.55 of Year 3.) This compares with the undiscounted payback period of 2.25 years (see above: 'Payback').

It should be obvious why using *discounted* cash flows will always lengthen the payback period. This refinement does not overcome

Table 5.9   Net present value of Project A, using a 12 per cent discount rate

End of year	Cash flow (£)	Discount factor	Present value (£)
0	−9,000	1.000	−9,000
1	+3,000	0.893	+2,679
2	+4,000	0.797	+3,188
3	+8,000	0.712	+5,696
Net present value			+2,653

the main objection to the payback method (namely, that it does not measure profitability); though if there is a finite period within which discounted payback is expected to be achieved, at least that implies that the net present value is positive.

Summary

In this chapter we have looked at several discounted cash flow methods:

- Net terminal value (NTV) and compounding to horizon (CH).
- Net present value (NPV).
- Profitability index (PI) and annualized cost (AC).
- Internal rate of return (IRR).
- Discounted payback.

Table 5.10 summarizes the various DCF methods we have discussed.

Table 5.10 Various DCF methods summarized and compared

	Pre-selected interest rate	Reinvestment assumption	Trial-and-error procedure	Rate-of-return solution
Discounted payback	Yes	n/a	No	No
Net terminal value (NTV)	Yes	Yes	No	No
Net present value (NPV)	Yes	Yes	No	No
Profitability index (PI)	Yes	Yes	No	No
Annualized cost (AC)	Yes	Yes	No	No
Compounding to horizon (CH)	Yes	Yes	Yes	Yes
Internal rate of return (IRR)	No	Implicit	Yes	Yes

6

Capital project appraisal refinements

Taxation

Writing-down allowances

Corporation tax is levied on **taxable profit** rather than on the profit which the accounts report. In computing taxable profit, depreciation of fixed assets charged in arriving at accounting profit is disallowed as an expense. Instead there are tax writing-down allowances (capital allowances) for certain kinds of capital spending.

The **writing-down allowance** reduces taxable profit and hence reduces tax payments. On plant and equipment, for example, the allowance is 25 per cent of cost in the year of purchase, and 25 per cent of the declining balance in each subsequent year (see Table 6.1).

There are special provisions for short-lived assets, such as computer hardware. If such assets are sold within five years, any surplus of the proceeds over the tax written-down value will be subject to a balancing charge. After five years, the asset's tax written-down value is transferred into the main pool of plant and equipment for subsequent wdas. For industrial buildings the annual writing-down allowance is 4 per cent of the cost of the new building (for 25 years). Offices, shops, and wholesale warehouses do not qualify for any tax allowances (except in enterprise zones).

Table 6.1 Writing-down allowances on plant and equipment (£'000)

Cost of equipment		250.0
Year 1 writing-down allowance (wda)	(25% of 250.0)	62.5
EOY 1 tax written-down value		187.5
Year 2 wda	(25% of 187.5)	46.9
EOY 2 tax written-down value		140.6
Year 3 wda		35.1
EOY 3 tax written-down value		105.5
Year 4 wda		26.4
EOY 4 tax written-down value		79.1
Year 5 wda		19.8
EOY 5 tax written-down value		59.3
Year 6 wda		14.8
EOY 6 tax written-down value		44.5

Corporation tax

The rate of corporation tax is 33 per cent for taxable profits above £1.5 million. On taxable profits up to £300,000 the tax rate is 25 per cent. (Between £300,000 and £1.5 million the marginal tax rate is 35 per cent.)

We need to estimate a capital project's tax effect on the whole company. Table 6.2 shows a company's extra tax payments resulting from a project requiring £250,000 investment in equipment. Extra revenue is £220,000 per year and expenses £120,000 per year (excluding book depreciation). Discounted at 10 per cent, and ignoring wdas after Year 5, the net present value of the tax cash flows amounts to −£60,700.

We assume the investment in equipment occurs in the year before any extra revenue arises. Where a project reduces taxable profit (as in Year 0 in Table 6.2) the company's overall tax bill will fall, assuming that the rest of the company has taxable profits against which to offset the allowances. This results in a positive tax cash inflow in Year 1. Companies not currently paying UK tax can carry forward losses or writing-down allowances for future use.

UK corporation tax is normally payable 9 months after the **financial year** end (or 15 months after the average point of earning

Table 6.2 Amount, timing, and present values of extra corporation tax (£'000)

	End of year						
	0	1	2	3	4	5	6
Capital expenditure	250						
Sales revenue	–	+220.0	+220.0	+220.0	+220.0	+220.0	–
Expenses (excluding depreciation)	–	−120.0	−120.0	−120.0	−120.0	−120.0	–
Margin	–	+100.0	+100.0	+100.0	+100.0	+100.0	–
Writing-down allowance	−62.5	−46.9	−35.1	−26.4	−19.8	−14.8	–
Taxable income	−62.5	+53.1	+64.9	+73.6	+80.2	+85.2	–
Corporation tax @ 33%	–	+20.6	−17.5	−21.4	−24.3	−26.5	−28.1
10% discount factor		0.909	0.826	0.751	0.683	0.621	0.564
Present values −60.7 =	–	+18.7	−14.4	−16.0	−16.6	−16.5	−15.9

Table 6.3 Assuming same-year tax payments at a tax rate discounted by one year (£'000)

	End of year						
	0	1	2	3	4	5	6
Taxable income	−62.5	+53.1	+64.9	+73.6	+80.2	+85.2	–
Tax @ 30% same year	+18.7	−15.9	−19.4	−22.1	−24.1	−25.6	–
10% discount factor	1.000	0.909	0.826	0.751	0.683	0.621	–
Present values −60.7	+18.7	−14.4	−16.0	−16.6	−16.5	−15.9	–

taxable profits); but ACT on dividends accelerates payment. As a rule we discount only at whole year intervals, and we normally assume that tax payments lag by a year. (That is why, in Table 6.2, the taxable profit in Year 5 gives rise to a tax payment in Year 6.)

In order to avoid the complication of the one-year time-lag in paying tax, Table 6.3 shows that we could get the same result by assuming a tax rate payable *in the same year* of 30 per cent. This is equivalent to using a corporation tax rate of '33 per cent discounted by 10 per cent' [i.e. $33.0 \times 0.909 = 30.0$].

Capital disinvestment

Why projects end

Capital **disinvestment** means reducing the assets a business holds. Possible limits to a project's life may stem from the following:

1. Physical exhaustion of equipment.
2. Technical obsolescence of equipment or process.
3. Market factors, such as changing consumer tastes.

A project's life may change after it has started. Sometimes a firm may need to abandon a project early, if conditions or estimates have changed – perhaps even before it comes on stream. One can compare the remaining NPV of the (continuing) project with the NPV of stopping it and selling the assets. Another option for self-contained projects might be to sell them as a *going* concern to another company.

Amounts recoverable at the end of a project's life may represent:

1. Value of land or buildings.
2. Scrap or second-hand value of equipment.
3. Working capital, such as stocks and debtors.

These items will appear as positive cash flows at the terminal date, together with any tax-related cash flows.

Even where a firm expects to recover part or all of its investment at the end of a project, the time value of money is still relevant. Capital has an opportunity cost as long as it is invested in a project: it could have been used for something else. So a firm must discount back to present value any amounts (**terminal values** or **residual values**) it expects to recover at the end.

In appraising long projects, it is normal to use an arbitrary **horizon** period of ten, or perhaps fifteen, years. Firms do not consider cash flows beyond the horizon, even if they expect the project to last longer. With a fairly high discount rate this makes little difference. (For example, with a 15 per cent a year discount rate, doubling the horizon period from fifteen to thirty years for a project with equal annual cash inflows would increase the present value of all the cash inflows by only 12½ per cent. The discount factor would increase from 5.847 to 6.566.)

Working capital

In addition to investment in fixed assets, many projects involving expansion or new products also involve investment in working capital, in stocks and debtors. This is less likely to be true for cost reduction projects.

Rather than show cash receipts from sales and cash payments for purchases, it is often easier to show sales revenues and **cost of goods sold (COGS)** as in the profit and loss account (but excluding depreciation); and then to show 'investment in working capital' as a

Table 6.4 Incremental cash flows from a project (£'000)

	End of year						
	0	1	2	3	4	5	6
Capital:							
Capital expenditure	−250.0					−*	
Corporation tax on wda		+20.6	+15.5	+11.6	+8.7	+6.5	+4.9
Stocks	−40.0					+40.0	
Debtors		−56.0				+56.0	
Creditors	+30.0					−30.0	
	−260.0	−35.4	+15.5	+11.6	+8.7	+72.5	+4.9
Revenue:							
Sales revenue		+220.0	+220.0	+220.0	+220.0	+220.0	
Expenses		−120.0	−120.0	−120.0	−120.0	−120.0	
Margin		+100.0	+100.0	+100.0	+100.0	+100.0	
Corporation tax on profits			−33.0	−33.0	−33.0	−33.0	−33.0
		+100.0	+67.0	+67.0	+67.0	+67.0	−33.0
Net cash flow	−260.0	+64.6	+82.5	+78.6	+75.7	+139.5	−28.1

*Note: In this case assuming no recovery of fixed capital at end.

separate amount. The timing of this investment may be a little complex.

Stocks in the form of raw materials, purchased parts, work-in-progress and finished goods need to be built up before any goods can be sold. (Purchases on credit may partly offset their cash flow impact.) Credit sales also imply an investment in debtors (accounts receivable); but this will be *after* the sales have been made. At the end of a project's life, stocks, debtors and creditors will fall to zero; though some stocks may have to be scrapped.

Table 6.4 shows the main types of incremental cash flows arising from a project involving an increase in sales revenue. The table separates **capital** and **revenue** items, and splits the net tax cash flows between them. The working capital part is inside the box. Note that the working capital items have no tax effects, since taxable profit is computed on an accruals basis.

Check that you can see where the Year 3 tax receipts of £11,600 and payments of £33,000 have come from. (Of course, together they equal the net payment of £21,400 in Table 6.2.)

Inflation

What inflation means

So far we have ignored the effects of inflation on the cash flows of capital projects. But in many countries inflation is too high to overlook (see Chapter 2). Given that many projects last for more than ten years, a 7 per cent annual rate of inflation implies that by the end of a project prices may be at least twice as high as at the start. (For a twenty-year project starting in 1970, the UK multiple would actually have been nearly *seven times!*)

General inflation means an increase in the average level of prices, as measured by the **retail prices index**. But one may often need to forecast *specific* price changes for component items in a capital project. Selling prices, material costs, wage rates – such prices may be critical for a project's success or failure. It will nearly always be too simplistic to assume that inflation will affect all items in the same way over a period of years.

Inflation is not just a technical detail affecting the numbers: it can have a profound impact on business projects. For example, if the UK has faster inflation than other countries, then sooner or later the pound will have to devalue against other currencies. Meanwhile there may be much uncertainty. A devaluation may have a major effect, for example, on export prices, cost of imported materials, and so on. Or high domestic inflation may lead in future, as it has in the not-so-distant past, to some form of general price control. This too can devastate business profits, since it often amounts to compelling firms to cut their prices in real terms. (Regulators are compelling some privatized utilities to do this at the moment.)

Inflation and tax

For tax purposes writing-down allowances are based on the original money cost of fixed assets: they are not adjusted for inflation. But, of course, if sales revenue or expenses increase as a result of inflation, that will affect the amount of corporation tax payable.

Example

To understand the impact of inflation on a project's net cash flows, let us look again at Table 6.2 (on page 78). Assume the cash flows for sales revenues and expenses need to be adjusted to allow for expected inflation of 10 per cent a year (cumulative from Year 0). We can recalculate in Table 6.5 the amount of the cash flows for corporation tax, using the format from Table 6.2.

Notice again the one-year time-lag between the taxable income and the related tax payment. You may like to verify that after the first tax cash flow (a receipt of £20,600 in Year 1), the other corporation tax payments are higher than the earlier amounts shown in Table 6.2. The increases reflect 33 per cent of the extra taxable

Table 6.5 Table 6.2's cash flows recalculated for 10 per cent a year inflation (£'000)

	End of year						
	0	1	2	3	4	5	6
Sales revenue	–	+242.0	+266.2	+292.8	+322.1	+354.3	–
Expenses	–	−132.0	−145.2	−159.7	−175.7	−193.3	–
Margin	–	+110.0	+121.0	+133.1	+146.4	+161.0	–
Writing-down allowance	−62.5	−46.9	−35.1	−26.4	−19.8	−14.8	–
Taxable income	−62.5	+63.1	+85.9	+106.7	+126.6	+146.2	–
Corporation tax @ 33%		+20.6	−20.8	−28.3	−35.2	−41.8	−48.2

income year by year, that is 33 per cent of: £10,000, £21,000, £33,100, £46,400, and £61,000. Thus the amounts of tax have increased by: £3,300, £6,900, £10,900, £15,300, and £20,100.

The writing-down allowances *have not changed* as a result of the 10 per cent a year inflation – being based by law on original money cost. So the amount of taxable income, and therefore the amount of tax payable, has not merely increased by 10 per cent a year. The effect of inflation on tax is not so simple!

Inflation and working capital

Working capital investment is also subject to inflation. Stock levels which stay constant in physical terms will require an increasing level of money investment. Likewise, if debtor days outstanding remain constant, the money investment in debtors will grow as selling prices increase. (And creditors will grow as supplier prices increase.) The extra working capital cash flow will be the increase (or decrease) in working capital compared to the previous year.

Example

Assume a five-year project involves a net investment of £10,000 in stocks less creditors at the end of Year 0, and of £56,000 in debtors at the end of Year 1 (as in Table 6.4). What is the amount of investment in working capital, and the resulting extra cash flow year by year, given an inflation rate of 10 per cent a year? (See Table 6.6.)

Table 6.6 Extra working capital needed, as a result of 10 per cent a year inflation (£'000)

	End of year					
	0	1	2	3	4	5
Stocks less creditors	10.0	11.0	12.1	13.3	14.6	–
Debtors	–	61.6	67.8	74.5	82.0	–
Total	10.0	72.6	79.9	87.8	96.6	–
Incremental cash flow	10.0	62.6	7.3	7.9	8.8	(96.6)
Per Table 6.4	10.0	56.0	–	–	–	(66.0)
Extra cash flow due to 10% inflation	–	6.6	7.3	7.9	8.8	(30.6)

The sum of all the cash flows is 0, because we assume that we recover all the investment in working capital in full at the end of Year 5. The essential point is that working capital 'held constant in real terms' still involves incremental money cash flows each year. We must allow for these *even* if we choose to set out the cash flows in 'real terms' not in money terms (see above).

How to cope with inflation

In principle, there are two ways to cope with inflation on discounted cash flow appraisal of capital investment projects. Perhaps the easiest to understand is to forecast all cash flows in money terms, allowing for specific price changes, and then to discount these future money amounts at a nominal (money) discount rate which *includes* an allowance for general inflation.

If the rate of inflation varies, it may be rather messy using a different discount rate from year to year over the life of the project (for the net present value method); and in fact few companies seem to do so. (It is, of course, not feasible to vary the discount rate using the internal rate of return method, whether between years or between different items in the same year.)

An alternative approach is to forecast specific money cash flows as above; then to discount *twice* – once to allow for general inflation, and then using a 'real discount rate' to allow for the real opportunity cost of capital. The starting point for computing a real discount rate may be the **yield to redemption** on index-linked gilt-edged securities, which represents the real risk-free rate of return (see Chapter 2).

The real discount rate should be lower than the money discount rate by the rate of inflation. For example, if the money discount rate is 15 per cent, but 4 per cent inflation is expected (which the 15 per cent presumably includes), then the real discount rate to use would be only 11 per cent. (Strictly speaking, it should be $1.15 \div 1.04 = 1.1058$ (i.e. 10.58 per cent), not $1.15 - 1.04 = 1.11$ (i.e. 11 per cent).)

In some ways it may seem less trouble to forecast cash flows in real terms (in effect, in terms of 'Year 0 pounds' throughout), and then just discount by the same real discount rate each year. But such an approach has three snags, as follows:

1. It is nearly always too simplistic to assume that inflation will affect all items to the same extent.

2. Writing-down allowances are based on original money cost. So, in times of inflation, they will be *falling* in real terms; and real cash flows must reflect that fact (which seems to be easy to overlook).

3. The cash flow impact of inflation on working capital is complex. Even if working capital seems to be constant in real terms (for example, the number of days' stock or number of days' debtors), there will still be a need for some extra cash flow investment in money terms. *This is not the same as a zero investment in real terms* (see above).

Table 6.7 illustrates the last two points. It repeats the items in Table 6.4, but assuming 10 per cent a year inflation. There are three reasons why the numbers in Table 6.7, even when discounted back into real terms, are not identical with the original numbers in Table 6.4.

1. The increase in working capital (in Year 0 £s) amounts to £900 for Year 1, and to £6,000 a year for Years 2 and 5. This, of course, is a real increase.

2. The writing-down allowances gradually lose value in real terms, being based on original money cost. The higher the inflation rate, the larger the real loss.

3. Tax on profits, being lagged by one year, is reduced in real terms by £3,000 a year from Years 2 to 6.

It will be clear that these adjustments are somewhat complex to work out. One needs to treat inflation with respect!

Risk and uncertainty

Risk and expected values

We can distinguish between **risk** and **uncertainty**. 'Risk' is where we *know* the chance of each possible outcome occurring (as in roulette or with dice). 'Uncertainty' exists where, as is usual in business, one can only estimate the odds (that is, guess).

Suppose that, for a new product, a firm reckons that annual sales levels of 400, 250, or 100 units are possible, and that the chances of

Table 6.7   Table 6.4's cash flows adjusted for 10 per cent a year inflation (£'000)

	End of year						
	0	1	2	3	4	5	6
Capital:							
Capital expenditure	−250.0						
Corporation tax on wda		+20.6	+15.5	+11.6	+8.7	+6.5	+4.9
Working capital	−10.0	−62.6	−7.3	−7.9	−8.8	+96.6	
	−260.0	−42.0	+8.2	+3.7	−0.1	+103.1	+4.9
Revenue:							
Sales revenue		+242.0	+266.2	+292.8	+322.1	+354.3	
Expenses		−132.0	−145.2	−159.7	−175.7	−193.3	
Margin		+110.0	+121.0	+133.1	+146.4	+161.0	
Corporation tax			−36.3	−39.9	−43.9	−48.3	−53.1
		+110.0	+84.7	+93.2	+102.5	+112.7	−53.1
Net cash flow	−260.0	+68.0	+92.9	96.9	+102.4	+215.8	−48.2
Discount factor (10%)	1.000	0.909	0.826	0.751	0.683	0.621	0.564
Net cash flow in year 0 £s	−260.0	+61.8	+76.8	+72.7	+69.9	+134.0	−27.2
Original cash flows per Fig. 6.4	−260.0	+64.6	+82.5	+78.6	+75.7	+139.5	−28.1
Difference	−	−2.8	−5.7	−5.9	−5.8	−5.5	+0.9
Consisting of:							
Working capital		−0.9	−6.0	−6.0	−6.0	−6.0	
Writing-down allowance		−1.9	−2.7	−2.9	−2.8	−2.5	−2.1
Tax on profits			+3.0	+3.0	+3.0	+3.0	+3.0

Table 6.8   Subjective probabilities and 'expected values'

Sales volume (£'000)	Estimated profit (£'000)	Estimated probability	'Expected' sales (£'000)	'Expected' profit (£'000)
400	130	0.1	40	13
250	40	0.6	150	24
100	(50)	0.3	30	(15)
		1.0	220	22

each outcome (in order) are 0.1, 0.6, and 0.3. By weighting the possible outcomes by their estimated chances of happening, we can calculate an '**expected value**' of sales volume of 220 units (see Table 6.8 opposite). We can do the same for the estimated profit at each possible level of sales, to arrive at an 'expected profit' of £22,000; and in principle we could use the same approach to compute an 'expected NPV' for the project, and make a decision on that basis.

Attaching subjective probabilities to uncertain future events allows arithmetical manipulation of the numbers. But that does not make the process 'scientific'. What confidence can we have in guesses about the chances of various outcomes? Can we even be sure we have considered every possible event? (Why should the probabilities add up to 1.0?) Experience suggests that events which in advance were thought quite impossible often seem afterwards to have been 'inevitable'. One might want to distinguish between possibilities that we considered in advance and rejected ('counter-expected') and those which we never imagined ('unexpected').

If we know the true odds, there is no uncertainty, only risk. But we are not safe in extrapolating frequencies for future events from statistics of past occurrences in similar cases. For we are then merely *assuming* that the past will repeat itself. But trends go on . . . until they stop! And what about unprecedented events? These are more typical of major business opportunities ('the chance of a lifetime'). What are the odds against California seceding from the United States of America before 2010?

When dealing with unique events we can never know if our estimate of the odds was correct – *even after the event!* It may sometimes be helpful to our thinking about a problem, to break it down into a number of simpler subproblems. This is the idea behind decision-tree analysis.

Uncertainty and sensitivity analysis

Business managers usually have to plan, control, and make decisions on the basis of uncertain estimates about the future. They may know some figures, such as suppliers' prices for the next few months, but about others they may feel very unsure. Where adverse events could badly damage their business, managers need to understand the range and likelihood of possible outcomes.

One way to try to cope is **sensitivity analysis**. The first step is often to make a single 'best estimate' ('best' = most likely) for each item. One might then also make 'optimistic' and 'pessimistic' estimates for each. The spreads may not be symmetrical: for instance, capacity constraints may prevent a firm from exceeding budgeted sales volume by much, whereas in a recession there could be a sharp decline.

Another approach is to vary the most likely estimate for each item in turn, to see how much it would affect the overall result. Some items will not matter much, even if they change by a large percentage. So one needs to identify the critical items, where even a fairly small percentage change could make quite a large difference to the overall result.

It is not much use to try changing each item by a fixed percentage (say 10 per cent); for some items could vary by much more, while others may be unlikely to change by nearly as much. A better method is to define an 'optimistic' estimate of income as one which there was only, say, a 1 in 10 chance of exceeding. (There would be only a 1 in 10 chance of falling short of the 'pessimistic' estimate of income.)

It is not easy to allow for interdependence among items, but it needs to be done. Merely to combine the pessimistic estimates of the most sensitive items would be far too gloomy. If 'pessimistic' means a 1 in 10 chance of a worst outcome, for example, with four completely independent variables, there would be only a 1 in 10,000 chance of such a combined outcome! Sensitivity analysis may help to answer the question, 'What if' – but it does not say how likely 'if' is.

Risk and the discount rate

When computing a project's NPV we have to preselect a discount rate which normally reflects the company's **weighted average cost of capital (WACC)** (see Chapter 10). Some companies use different discount rates for different types of project, to allow for differences in risk. For example, cost reduction projects may be regarded as low risk, and new product projects as high risk. (Conversely, one large company uses a *lower* discount rate for certain high-risk technical projects, as a deliberate safeguard against being left behind in the technology race.) How much to adjust the 'average' discount rate to allow for high- or low-risk projects is hard to judge.

The same might be done for different periods or for different kinds of cash flow. For example, the expected cash flow resulting from tax writing-down allowances on capital expenditure may be a good deal less uncertain than cash inflows estimated from future sales revenues. This could be allowed for by discounting the tax

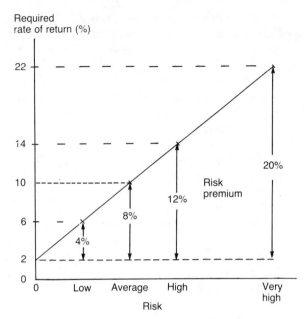

Figure 6.1 Required real rates of return for various levels of 'risk'

benefits at a lower rate (with a smaller risk premium), and thus, in effect, (present) valuing them more highly.

No method of estimating the cost of equity capital is precisely accurate. Over the years, the stock market has yielded average returns on equities of about 8 per cent a year more than on risk-free securities (gilts). Hence we may regard 8 per cent as the required risk premium to apply to capital investment in the average project. For a lower-risk project, a risk premium of (say) only about 4 per cent might be suitable; for an above-average-risk project, a risk premium of perhaps 12 per cent; and for a very high-risk project, a risk premium of as much as 20 per cent. These are, of course, crude and arbitrary guesses. If one adopted them, and if the real risk-free rate of return were 2 per cent, then Figure 6.1 shows the real required rates of return for projects of varying risks. (See also Figure 2.5 and Figure 10.2.)

Options

Managers often value flexibility – 'keeping their options open' – and Table 6.9 (below) lists a number of ways for them to reduce uncertainty. In the finance literature, **'options'** usually refer to derivatives of other assets, whether securities, currencies, commodities, or whatever. But they may merely mean 'flexibility' in a broader sense.

In general, a call option (an option to buy at a definite price within some future period) will increase in value the greater the volatility of the value of the underlying asset, and the longer the time period involved. Why is increased volatility valuable, if investors are risk-averse? Because since the holder can always choose not to exercise the option, he ignores downside risk. Thus the only relevant volatility is 'upside risk' – and the more of this the better!

Some kinds of real options may be relevant for managers making capital investment decisions, including: the possibility of investing (more) in future, after the outcome of a particular event has become less uncertain; or of abandoning a project if results are unsatisfactory. These 'options' are difficult to value with basic DCF techniques, because the various possible outcomes affect the proper discount rate to use. Some kind of decision-tree approach may be most suitable.

Managing uncertainty

'Business risk' refers to how a business invests its resources, **'financial risk'** to how it *finances* them. Borrowing to finance assets is risky because the business must legally make regular interest payments and must repay the amount borrowed on the due date. For any fluctuation in operating profits (before interest), such financial gearing increases the volatility (= risk) of the profits for equity shareholders. In contrast, equity capital is less risky for the business, since it implies no legal commitments in terms of dividends or capital repayments (see Chapters 7 and 8).

A firm can reduce business risk in a number of ways. Table 6.9, which is certainly not comprehensive, lists three kinds of business actions: contractual, flexible, and uncertainty-reducing. Some actions may either reduce risk or increase it, such as diversifying into different (less familiar) businesses, or building spare capacity.

A survey of 146 large UK companies (Ho *et al.*, 1991) found that about 40 per cent often or very often used sensitivity analysis, 39 per cent a subjective/intuitive assessment of risk, and 17 per cent probability analysis. Methods of adjusting for risk (of the 133 companies that did so) most frequently included raising the required rate of return (42 per cent), shortening the payback period (34 per

Table 6.9 Ways of reducing uncertainty

	Contractual	Flexible	Uncertainty-reducing
Sales	Produce goods only against firm orders, not for stock	Avoid overdependence on a few customers or products	Extensive market research before launching new products
Purchases	Arrange long-term supply contracts	Arrange more than one source of supply	Stockpile raw materials
Assets	Insure as much as possible	Use general-purpose rather than highly specialized equipment	Retain high liquid resources
Employees	Contract work out rather than using full-time employees	Pay partly by commission or bonus rather than flat rate	Promote from within rather than hire from outside

cent), and adjusting estimated future cash flows subjectively/ intuitively (63 per cent).

Capital budgeting

Organization

In addition to a method of looking at each project's future cash flows, companies need a system of **capital budgeting**. This involves planning aggregate **capital expenditure** over the next year or two, and splitting it into quarterly totals which form part of the cash budget. This helps to arrange suitable financing in good time.

Both the amount and the timing of capital projects can change quickly. Business conditions may make it desirable either to speed up or to slow down capital spending. In extreme cases firms may have to cancel projects even after they have been started, though this can be very expensive.

Capital spending takes *time*. This, as much as limited finance, may account for companies imposing **capital rationing**. Even if Railtrack, for example, had access to unlimited finance, completing all the projects they would like would still take several years.

Capital investment projects may be very large and may have important strategic implications, so businesses tend to be cautious about capital spending. Once under way, projects are often not reversible. For much specialized plant and equipment there may be no second-hand market, and even a potential buyer might only offer a low price.

That is why companies look carefully before they leap, and insist on thorough procedures for capital project proposals to pass through before approval. The larger the amount of money involved, or the greater the strategic importance, the higher up the organization a project must go for approval. Such approval may sometimes seem to be merely 'rubber-stamping', but this is probably because extensive informal discussions have already taken place before the formal submission of the project. In most organizations, what goes on informally is at least as important as the formal system. The internal politics of capital budgeting can be crucial.

Evaluation before and after

Table 6.10 summarizes the results of a 1986 survey of 100 large UK firms (Pike *et al.*, 1988). It shows that by no means all large UK companies use discounted cash flow methods at all; and those that do may also often use one or both of the simpler methods noted in Chapter 5.

Table 6.11 compares methods used for looking at capital projects in advance and those used for business performance appraisal after the event. Clearly there are several differences. It has been suggested that using cash flows as the basis for ex post performance appraisal (rather than accounting profits) could avoid many of the differences. The asterisks in Table 6.11 show which way cash flow accounting would probably tend.

Items 1a and 4 would remain difficult points to overcome. After the event it may often be very hard to identify incremental amounts

Table 6.10   Popular capital investment appraisal methods

	Frequency of use in 1986 in 100 large UK firms				
	Total	Always	Mostly	Often	Rarely
Payback	92	47	24	16	5
Internal rate of return	75	42	13	11	9
Net present value	68	23	14	15	16
Average accounting rate of return	56	18	10	15	13

Table 6.11 Ex ante project appraisal versus ex post performance appraisal

In advance	After the event
Main methods: NPV, IRR	Main methods: RI, ROI
1a Incremental amounts 1b Relating to discrete 'projects' 1c Over all (or most) of project's life	*1a Overall totals *1b Relating to whole business unit *1c For a single period (often one year)
*2a Cash flows *2b Ignoring depreciation *2c After tax	2a Profits (or losses) 2b After charging depreciation 2c Often before tax

3a May be constant purchasing
      power units (= Year 0 money)
3b Often discounted
3c Implicit reinvestment assumption
	*3a Usually monetary units (distorted
	      by inflation)
	*3b Not discounted
	*3c No reinvestment assumption

4 Uncertainty clearly relevant	4 Uncertainty often ignored

Note: * indicates which way cash-flow accounting would probably tend.

resulting from projects which the ongoing business has thoroughly absorbed. (This is a major problem in post-project audits: see below.) Nor will it be possible to make useful guesses after the event about the actual degree of risk involved. (Of course, this is not easy *before* the event either!)

Figure 6.2 illustrates point 1 in Table 6.11: the contrast between looking at incremental amounts relating to discrete projects over a project's whole life, and looking at overall totals relating to the whole business unit for a single accounting period.

Post-project audits

Some larger companies arrange **post-project audits** for some of their capital projects. As soon as a project is on stream, one can check the amount and the timing of the capital spending. But the audit may be more ambitious and review operating cash flows too.

Normally such audits take place when a project may still have most of its life to run. It would make little sense to wait until a ten-year project was over. Conditions would have changed too much, the people involved might have moved on, and any lessons might be out of date. Thus an audit may take place after a project has been running for, say, one year. Original estimates can be

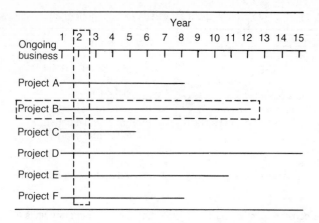

Figure 6.2 Project lives and accounting periods

compared with actual outcomes for capital spending and perhaps for the first year of operations. But for later years, any comparison may simply be with more recent estimates.

A post-project audit need not be entirely backward-looking. It may sometimes be possible to reassess a project's future as a result. Probably only larger projects or projects with problems will be subject to audit. It may not be easy to measure a project's impact after the event, nor its 'riskiness'.

That implies a need to specify the purpose of post-project audits. It might be dangerous, as well as demotivating, to try to allocate blame where things have gone wrong. That might induce a risk-averse attitude in managers. It is probably more useful to aim to learn what went right and what did not; and how to do better in future. Important aspects of a project to review might include: capital spending, assumptions about market size and market share, operating costs, the timing of events, estimates of project life, and so forth.

References

Ho, S. S. M. and Pike, R. H. (1991), 'Risk analysis in capital budgeting contexts: simple or sophisticated?', *Accounting and Business Research*, no. 83, summer, 227–38.

Pike, R. H. and Wolfe, M. (1988), 'Capital budgeting in the 1990s', *Management Accounting*, October, 28–30.

7

Borrowing

General features

Background

A company must repay amounts borrowed ('debt') as they become
due ('mature'), and pay the regular agreed amount of interest on the
debt outstanding. Failure to do so entitles the lender to take legal
action at once to recover the principal and any unpaid interest. Both
lender and borrower will want to see a good margin of safety. Then
they can both be confident that a company can meet its legal
commitments even if things don't go quite as planned.

A lender will be concerned with the borrower's honesty and
competence. The borrower will have to say *why* he needs the
money, how much he requires, and for how long. He must also
explain how he expects to be able to repay the loan in due course.
Detailed cash forecasts covering (at least) the whole period of the
proposed loan may help to answer many of these important
questions. It may be useful to prepare more than one set of
forecasts, based on different assumptions, to give an idea of the
margin for error.

A firm's financial director or managing director should be sure to
talk to the bank manager at least once a year. If everything is going
well, this regular discussion may simply amount to a friendly chat.
It will keep the bank abreast of general trends, challenges and
opportunities currently facing the business. If there are financial

95

problems, there may be a need for longer and more detailed meetings.

In addition, the business should keep the bank manager informed of its financial progress, at a minimum sending the bank the firm's annual accounts. It might also be sensible to send a copy of the cash forecasts for the ensuing year. Unfortunately some businesses do not prepare such forecasts on any formal basis even for their own internal use. Needless to say, they are the ones most likely to find themselves suddenly in need of 'unexpected' bank borrowing. (What bad luck! – it was Gary Player who remarked that he found the more he practised, the 'luckier' he became!)

Events may cause any business, however well run, to want to borrow money from time to time. Of course, one cannot forecast the precise dates and amounts of unpredictable borrowing requirements. There may be some truth in describing a banker as 'someone who will lend you money only when you don't need it'. It makes sense, therefore, for a business to be on good terms with its bank. It is when you do not need the money that you can lay the foundations for subsequent borrowing. If the need does arise later, there may then be a fair chance of being able to borrow the amount required on acceptable terms.

Short-term borrowing

A bank overdraft is a popular form of short-term borrowing which is convenient and flexible for borrowers. Its main drawback is that it is legally repayable 'on demand', hence balance sheets show overdrafts as current liabilities. Only the amount actually overdrawn bears interest, though there may be a small 'commitment fee' on the agreed maximum limit. Interest accrues from day to day, at a rate which can vary with market conditions.

Term loans range from periods of less than a year to more than five years. They may provide for borrowing in tranches, and for repayment by instalments (rather than a single 'bullet' repayment on maturity). In **project finance** the timing of repayment may depend on a project's profitability. Term loans may be more expensive than overdrafts, often with a penalty on early repayment, which can limit flexibility. Term loans are normally variable-rate, because high and volatile rates of inflation make fixed-rate loans risky both for lenders and for borrowers. Longer-term loans often carry higher interest rates than short-term borrowings (see Chapter 2). And smaller or riskier firms will have to pay higher rates of interest than larger or more secure borrowers.

Also included among current liabilities may be parts of loans originally arranged for more than one year. This may be the entire principal of a loan now nearly due; or it may comprise a part of the total amount, for example of finance leases (see below). For purposes of calculating gearing (see Chapter 10), it is probably best to include in total 'debt' all negotiated interest-bearing finance, both short-term and long-term.

Long-term borrowing

Long-term loans to companies (often called **debentures**, from the Latin 'they are owed') may be with or without **security** (see below). The borrower of a long-term loan must repay the whole amount on the maturity date. A company whose financial position has worsened may find it hard to repay a loan or to arrange new borrowing ('refinance'). Inability to repay debt is one of the main causes of corporate failure. In order to reduce the risk, some kinds of project finance may provide for partial repayment at regular intervals.

Divisions of a large group often plan investment in fixed assets themselves, but borrowing is usually arranged centrally by the whole group. This is partly to reduce the lender's risk, since the whole group's assets, not just a single division's, will then be available to cover the loan. Also to benefit from economies of scale it makes sense to concentrate borrowing expertise in a single group treasury department.

The 1980 Wilson Committee, in respect of large and medium-sized companies, 'could not find a single example of an investment project which had not gone ahead because of the inability to raise external finance . . .'. It expressed no view about whether banks tended to be overcautious with respect to gearing and security conditions for small firms. The conclusion is that for larger firms the capital market is probably very effective; but this may be less true for small firms.

The stock exchange may 'list' loans to larger companies, just like government borrowings. The original lender can then be 'repaid', in effect, not by the corporate borrower, but by selling his **loan stock** to another investor. At the maturity date the borrowing company will repay the principal amount to the current holders of the loan stock. (Some companies start to buy in their own loan stock towards the **redemption** date to reduce the total amount of cash needed on final maturity.) Smaller firms may arrange loans from banks, insurance companies, pension funds, or private investors. With only a single lender it may be possible to renegotiate certain loan conditions if circumstances change. That is not feasible with listed loan stocks which are held by widely dispersed members of the public.

Companies with overseas assets may choose to borrow in foreign currencies rather than in sterling. The interest rate payable may be different from UK interest rates, depending mainly on the expected relative rates of inflation. The sterling exchange rate may change during the period of the loan; in which case the true cost of such borrowing comprises the interest payable plus or minus any loss or gain on exchange. (The tax effects may be significant here.) Borrowing in foreign currencies can be risky if overseas earnings do not fully cover the interest and principal. This was a significant reason why Laker Airways collapsed in the early 1980s.

Reducing the lender's risk

General considerations

Lenders will be concerned with the margin of safety. In particular:

- How far might profits and cash generation fall in a downturn?
- To what extent could the company reduce planned spending at lower levels of output?
- How quickly could the borrower liquidate current assets if need be to pay loan interest or to repay principal?
- How quickly could fixed assets be sold off in a crisis? How marketable are they? How low at worst could their second-hand values be, if the whole industry is depressed?

Is the *borrower* both honest and competent? What is his track record? What about his character: would a possible default really concern him? If his financial position were to get much worse, would he continue to provide regular accurate up-to-date reports?

What sort of *business* is it? Profitable? Risky? How good is the management, especially financial management and management **control**? Is there adequate depth of management?

Personal guarantees

In a **limited company** the liability of the shareholders is *limited* (hence the name) to the nominal amount of the issued ordinary share capital. In contrast, the creditors of **partnerships** or sole traders ('unincorporated' businesses) can, if need be, look for repayment to the private assets of the individual proprietors (owners), *in addition* to any assets of the firm itself. Thus the potential liability of sole owners or partners in a firm is *unlimited* (in the same way as for 'names' at Lloyds).

A small business is likely to be risky; so anyone lending money to a small limited company may want to get a personal **guarantee** of repayment from the main shareholders. This will put the lender in the same position as if the company were a sole trader or partnership.

The reverse side of this coin is that giving a personal guarantee is a major step. At the time it may seem almost like a 'free' way of improving a small company's credit rating. But giving a personal guarantee *fundamentally* changes the legal position of whoever gives it (whether the controlling owner, a director or a friend or relative). If things go wrong, the consequences may be extremely serious. 'Caveat emptor' ('let the buyer beware') may nowadays not have quite the weight it once carried; but 'caveat guarantor' is still essential advice.

Security

Another way for a lender to reduce his risk of loss is to arrange for certain assets to serve as formal **collateral** for the loan. On liquidation of the business this gives him priority: the proceeds from selling those assets will go first to repay his **secured loan**. Anything left over will go into the company's general pool of funds to pay other, unsecured, creditors. What if the proceeds from selling assets serving as collateral do not cover the full amount of a secured loan? To the extent of any shortfall, the creditor will rank as unsecured.

Debtors, some kinds of stocks, and general equipment can serve as collateral for loans, as well as land, buildings, and marketable investments. For highly specialized assets there may be no resale market. Legal title to the asset needs to be easily transferable; and the asset's value should be fairly stable and easy to determine. It should also cover the amount of any loan by a fair margin.

Instead of securing a loan on specific assets, a lender may obtain a **floating charge** on all a borrower's assets. This comes into effect ('crystallizes') only if a company goes into liquidation – and thus permits the sale of assets in the normal course of business. (An asset which is serving as security for a loan can be sold only if the lender agrees.) On a winding up, certain debts (for example, certain wages and taxes) come before the claims of unsecured creditors. They also have priority over any floating charges – though *not* over a fixed charge on a specific asset.

Covenants

Corporate lenders usually insist on certain conditions (**covenants**). Their main functions are as follows:

1. To prevent the sale of substantial parts of the business, or the granting of prior claims on assets to other subsequent lenders.
2. To require the maintenance of certain financial ratios at stated levels, or the maintenance of physical assets in good condition.
3. To assure the provision of regular up-to-date financial information.
4. (For smaller companies) to restrict the amount of directors' salaries or dividend payments.

Breaches of covenant (like failure to pay interest when due) can entitle the lender to require immediate repayment of the loan. But a breach may simply act as a 'trigger': it alerts the lender to an unexpected event, and suggests a need to discuss the current state of the business with the borrower.

The cost of debt

The direct cost of borrowing is the payment of interest to the lender. Debt interest is an allowable expense in computing tax on company profits, so the after-tax cost of debt is usually less than the nominal rate of interest. If a company pays loan interest of 10 per cent a year, and if corporation tax on profits is 33 per cent, then the after-tax cost of debt is 6.7 per cent a year:

$$10\% \times (100\% - 33\%) = 10\% \times 67\% = 6.7\%$$

A loan to a higher-risk small company might cost 12 per cent a year, to include a larger risk premium. If that company were subject only to the 25 per cent 'small company' tax rate on profits, the debt's after-tax cost would be 9.0 per cent a year – an increase of about one third:

$$12\% \times (100\% - 25\%) = 12\% \times 75\% = 9.0\%$$

The tax laws refer to money, so the real gain to the borrower in respect of inflation is *not taxable*. The overall nominal rate of interest charged on a loan ex ante incorporates an inflation premium. For simplicity, the following example assumes that this turns out to be precisely correct when measured against the actual rate of inflation ex post. To calculate what the actual real rate of after-tax interest turned out to be after the event, it is the actual rate of inflation that needs to be taken into account – which may be very different from what was anticipated.

Example
Suppose a 10 per cent annual loan interest rate comprises the following:

- 4 per cent pure time preference;
- 4 per cent inflation premium (assumed correct); and
- 2 per cent risk premium.

Then the purchasing power needed to repay the loan will be 4/104 (= 3.9 per cent) a year less than originally borrowed. The tax system allows a company borrower to deduct from taxable profits all the money interest paid; but the borrowing company is *not* taxed on the 'real' gain resulting from the actual inflation. Hence the after-tax real cost can be very small. Given high enough inflation it could even be negative.

Table 7.1 includes three columns, to show the real after-tax cost of

Table 7.1 Real rates of after-tax interest

	Rate of inflation		
	4%	12%	20%
Before-tax interest rate	10.0	18.0	26.0
Less: corporation tax @ 33%	3.3	6.0	8.7
After-tax interest rate	6.7	12.0	17.3
Less: purchasing power gain	3.9	10.7	16.7
Real after-tax interest rate	2.8	1.3	0.6

loans whose nominal interest rate comprises 4 per cent pure time preference plus a 2 per cent risk premium plus different inflation premiums (in each case, for convenience, assumed correct) of 4 per cent, 12 per cent, and 20 per cent.

Other types of debt

Leases

Leases allow the lessee use of an asset in return for regular payments of lease rentals to the lessor, who remains the legal owner. **Operating leases** are short-term and often for small amounts and the lease rentals are simply treated as expenses. In contrast non-cancellable **financial leases** normally cover almost the whole of an asset's useful life. In effect, financial leases put the lessee in almost the same position as if he had borrowed and purchased the asset outright. So the lessee's balance sheet **capitalizes** financial leases and shows fixed assets matched by long-term 'liabilities'. Part of each year's lease rental is treated as interest expense, and part as repayment of the liability. (In addition, depreciation is charged on the fixed asset.) A similar approach applies to **hire-purchase** deals, where following a 20 per cent down payment, assets are acquired by instalments over up to five years.

In capital project appraisals, either future financial lease payments should be discounted at a very low discount rate (suitable for a debt-equivalent) or else they should be replaced by a 'payment' at the start of the project equivalent to the capital cost of the asset. In either case, tax reliefs on the lease payments need to be taken into account.

Income bonds

Income bonds are debt instruments on which (tax-deductible) interest is payable only if earned in the period, though missed interest payments are accumulated and made up later. Some people argue that income bonds offer all the advantages of preference share capital (see below), together with the tax advantages of debt. Income bonds must be redeemed by the issuer at a fixed amount on a specific date.

Convertible loans

Some long-term loans may be **convertible** into ordinary shares at the holder's option on prearranged terms. As long as a loan is not converted, it counts as **debt** on the balance sheet. It continues to incur regular interest payments, and ranks as a creditor in the event of winding-up. But upon conversion it ceases to bear interest, and becomes ordinary share capital ranking for dividends. The **option** to take up equity if the company prospers may reduce the nominal interest rate payable on convertible loan stocks. Where it makes much difference, earnings per share and book value of equity per share may be computed in two ways: both as they are now, and as they would be on a **fully diluted** basis.

Preference share capital

As a form of corporate finance, **preference share capital** lies 'in between' long-term borrowing and ordinary share capital. From a financial point of view many of its features are similar to debt, but legally it forms part of shareholders' funds. FRS 4 requires shareholders' funds to be analyzed between 'equity' – which would basically be ordinary share capital – and 'non-equity' – which would certainly include preference share capital. Debt interest must be paid before there can be any question of declaring preference dividends; and until a company has repaid lenders in full on winding-up, the preference shareholders will get nothing back at all. But preference capital has priority over ordinary capital, both with respect to dividends and with respect to ultimate capital repayment.

Mainly because they are not deductible for tax purposes, preference dividends are usually more expensive for a company to pay than debt interest. Failure to pay preference dividends will prevent payment of any ordinary dividends. No company contemplates that except in dire crisis, so in practice preference dividends may seem nearly as much a commitment as debt interest. Yet if the worst comes to the worst there is a big difference between a company being highly embarrassed if it has to omit preference dividends for a period or two, and being *liquidated* if it fails to pay interest on its debt.

As Figure 7.1 suggests, it may be better to view preference capital as an alternative to ordinary share capital (B), not to borrowing (A): as a useful way to increase financial gearing without too much risk. Indeed, preference shares will be much cheaper than ordinary

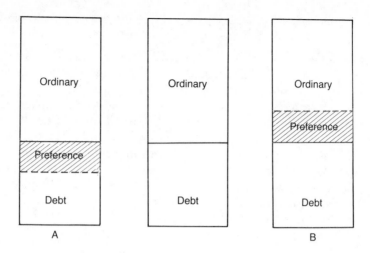

Figure 7.1   Alternative views of preference capital

shares (being so much less risky to the holders), yet (from the company's viewpoint) much less risky than debt.

Provisions for liabilities and charges

UK accounting standards require accounts to charge **deferred taxation** as an expense 'to the extent that it is probable that a liability will crystallize' in the foreseeable future. Deferred taxation: does not bear interest; is not a legal liability on the balance sheet date (merely the 'other side' of the amount charged in the profit and loss account); and (like the amount shown for pensions) is *not* normally regarded as part of a company's total negotiated debt. Other provisions may include pensions and provisions for restructuring (often arising on acquisition).

Valuing debt

Risk-free securities

About 75 per cent in value of all stock exchange transactions in the United Kingdom is in government (**gilt-edged**) securities. These are regarded as 'risk-free' (see Chapter 2). This market is important because it reflects expected future interest rates. We have seen how critical these are in many financial decisions.

The government issues new gilts for periods varying from three months to more than twenty-five years. Certain outstanding gilts have *no* redemption date – they are **irredeemable**, and simply promise to pay a stated coupon rate each year for ever. Some of these perpetuities have been in issue for more than 100 years, so they allow long-term comparisons of gilt-edged prices and risk-free interest rates. The **coupon rates** on outstanding gilts vary widely, mainly as a result of different interest rates on the various dates of issue.

In Chapter 5 we saw how to 'value' future cash flows from a capital investment project, by discounting them back to 'present value'. We can use exactly the same approach to value shares or other assets.

Imagine a risk-free government **security**, paying interest of £4 per £100 nominal of stock, once a year for ever (a **perpetuity**). Ignoring tax, what would we expect its market price (or present value) to be? We assume we know the amount and timing of all future cash receipts. The only other thing we need to find out is what interest rate to use to discount them back to present value. The proper discount rate to use is the 'opportunity cost' – the rate of return which could be earned on similar-risk (in this case, risk-free) investments.

Example

If the current interest yield on perpetual risk-free securities is 5.0 per cent a year, then the present value of '£4 a year for ever' should be £80 – since this gives the required interest yield of 5.0 per cent (= £4/£80). To find the capital value of a perpetuity, we simply divide the annual amount of the interest by the appropriate interest rate. In this case £4/0.05 = £80.

If the relevant interest rate were now to rise to 8 per cent a year, investors would sell the £4-a-year perpetuity until its market price reached £50 (=£4/0.08). At that point it would just yield the current rate of interest of 8 per cent (=£4/£50). Why would people sell the £4-a-year perpetuity if its market price were above £50? Because they would then be able to acquire – risk-free – a *larger* annual income for ever. Suppose the market price remained at £80. By selling the perpetuity, and reinvesting the £80 proceeds in a risk-free security yielding the 'going' rate of interest of 8 per cent a year, someone could achieve an income of £6.40 a year for ever (= 8 per cent × £80).

Table 7.2 Current market values for varying coupon rates and maturities, given a going rate of interest of 7 per cent a year

		Coupon rate		
		£3½	£7	£14
Redemption	0 years	100	100	100
	5	86	100	129
	15	68	100	164
	25	59	100	182
	Never	50	100	200

Suppose the term structure of interest rates were absolutely flat, at 7 per cent a year whatever the maturity of the stock. We know that a *perpetuity* carrying a coupon rate of 14 per cent would be priced in the market at £200; while a perpetuity with a coupon of 3½ per cent would be priced at £50. But what about stocks with a definite maturity date?

If the maturity date were *tomorrow*, then the market price would obviously be very close to £100 (the nominal amount repayable at maturity). That would be true whatever the coupon rate. But if the maturity date were exactly fifteen years in the future, then today's market price would be different for the two stocks. The 3½ per cent stock would be valued at about £68; while the 14 per cent stock would be valued at about £164. In each case that would give a **redemption yield** of the relevant rate of interest of 7 per cent, taking into account both the annual interest payments and the ultimate £100 receivable on maturity in fifteen years' time. (The contrast is with a *flat yield*, which simply represents the annual interest divided by the current market price.)

Table 7.2 also shows what the market value of each stock would be if redemption were in five years and twenty-five years.

Corporate debt

Valuing corporate debt is very like valuing risk-free securities, except that companies – even large ones – are normally riskier to lend to than governments. Hence the required rate of interest will include a risk premium, though it may be fairly small.

Again ignoring tax, suppose with the current risk-free rate of interest being 7 per cent a year (across all maturity dates – giving a flat term structure), BIG plc can borrow at 9 per cent a year – that is, with a 2 per cent a year risk premium. Let us suppose the coupon rate is 14 per cent, as the borrowing was undertaken when interest rates were much higher than they are now.

If the loan were repayable tomorrow, it would stand at almost par – say, £100 value per £100 nominal of loan stock. If the loan were a perpetuity, it would stand at £156, giving a yield of 9 per cent a year (= £14/156). If the loan were repayable in fifteen years' time, its value would be about £140. All we are doing is discounting back to present value the expected future cash receipts – both regular interest and ultimate repayment of principal – using the appropriate discount rate, which in this case is 9 per cent a year. If the perceived riskiness of the loan were to increase, the required risk premium would also rise – say, from 2 to 3 per cent a year. Then the appropriate discount rate would also rise (in this case from 9 per cent to 10 per cent), and the market value of the loan stock would fall (in this case for a fifteen-year maturity, roughly from £140 to £130).

It should be obvious that the market price of long-term loans will be more sensitive to a change in interest rates than the market price of short-term loans (if it isn't, look again at Table 7.2).

Deep discount bonds

Debt normally carries a coupon rate close to the current rate of interest (for the maturity) at the date of issue. But sometimes securities are issued which pay no interest at all during their life (zero coupon), or perhaps only a very low rate. The amount due on redemption then has to cover not merely the 'principal', but also the interest which has accrued during the life of the **deep discount bond**.

Table 7.3 Build-up of cumulative interest on a deep discount bond

End of year	Interest charged in year (£'000)	Liability at end of year (£'000)
0	–	5,000
1	500	5,500
2	550	6,050
3	605	6,655
4	665.50	7,320.50
5	732.05	(8,052.55)

For instance, suppose the current interest rate (ignoring tax) is 10 per cent a year; and a company borrows £5 million cash for five years, with no interest payable until redemption. The cash due at the end of Year 5 will be £8,052,550. The interest cumulating each year (on the start-of-year amount outstanding), and the 'liability' shown on the balance sheet at the end of each year, will be as shown in Table 7.3. The 'deep discount', in this case, merely represents the interest which is being deferred (or 'rolled up') until the final redemption date at the end of five years.

8

Ordinary shares

Shareholders' funds

The nature of ordinary shares

From the company's viewpoint, ordinary share capital (**equity**) is less risky than borrowing (debt) as a source of funds, for three main reasons.

1. There is no legal commitment to pay any dividend (unlike debt interest).
2. As long as the company exists it need never repay equity capital to shareholders, whereas it must repay loans on the due date.
3. Equity capital is free from the restrictions which lenders often attach to debt (see Chapter 7).

For shareholders it is the other way round: owning ordinary shares is more risky than lending a company money. On a **winding-up**, ordinary shareholders will get anything that remains after the company has repaid all other suppliers of finance in full. So in a successful company the potential reward to ordinary shareholders is limitless. But if the company cannot pay all creditors in full, then ordinary shareholders get nothing. In a limited company, however, the company cannot call on ordinary shareholders to subscribe any more money; once the shares are fully paid-up, the most they can lose is what they have already invested.

In theory dissatisfied shareholders may vote to replace a company's directors at the annual general meeting. But in practice they will usually simply sell their shares. The trouble is that by then the market value may already have fallen, to reflect past performance and poor future prospects. Large shareholders, in contrast, may prefer to remain and try to find ways to get the managers to improve the company's performance. (There have been some recent cases where financial institutions with large shareholdings in troubled companies have arranged, in conjunction with non-executive directors, to replace the chief executive.)

In **unlisted companies** it may be very difficult to influence a company's policy or to sell the shares. In fact outside equity capital is likely to be difficult and expensive for small companies, and probably available at all only to the most successful and promising ventures.

Ordinary shareholders' funds in accounts

The Companies Act 1985 sets out five headings under 'Capital and Reserves' (shareholders' funds):

1. Called up share capital.
2. Share premium account.
3. Revaluation reserve.
4. Other reserves.
5. Profit and loss account.

For most companies this boils down to three kinds of item:

1. Amounts received for new shares issued.
2. Revaluations of fixed assets.
3. Retained profits.

For practical purposes there is little point in splitting amounts received for new shares between the **nominal amount** per share and any **share premium**. In both cases it normally amounts to permanent capital. But one does need to distinguish between ordinary and preference shares, both of which legally count as shareholders' funds. Ordinary shares are '**equity**'; preference shares are 'non-equity'.

Revaluations of fixed assets mainly comprise the following:

1. Increases above cost in the book value of land and buildings (or, less commonly, plant and equipment).
2. Adjustments resulting from changes in foreign exchange rates.
3. (Negative) write-offs of acquired **goodwill**.

Revaluations of fixed assets (whether up or down) do not directly affect a company's finances – the **revaluation reserves** are 'merely' bookkeeping entries. They may affect depreciation charges (either up or down), but in the United Kingdom there are unlikely to be any tax consequences. But they will affect certain financial ratios, such as **debt ratio** and **return on equity**. Any downward revaluations to current assets would normally be charged as an expense in the profit and loss account.

Retained profits comprise the cumulative total to date of profit available for ordinary shareholders (profit after tax *less* minority interests and preference dividends) *less* ordinary **net dividends** paid and payable. For most companies this is probably a more important source of finance than either new issues of ordinary shares or borrowing.

The stock exchange

Economic functions

The stock exchange is a market on which investors can buy and sell securities of leading British and international companies, and of governments. In March 1994 there were about 100 different British government securities outstanding with a total market value of some £160 billion (with a *daily* turnover of £6.7 billion!). UK-listed shares of about 1,850 companies had a market value of about £720 billion.

The trend of the past thirty-five years shows a decline (mainly for tax reasons) in the proportion of listed equities held by individuals, and an increase in that held by insurance companies, pension funds, unit trusts and investment trusts (see Figure 1.2).

The main function of **unit trusts** and **investment trusts** is to invest in ordinary shares on behalf of individuals, who thus get the benefit of expert management and lower dealing costs, and perhaps a diversified **portfolio** (see Chapter 9). A unit trust is 'open-ended': it

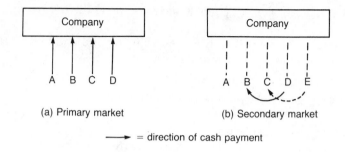

(a) Primary market   (b) Secondary market

⟶ = direction of cash payment

Figure 8.1   The stock exchange: primary and secondary markets

can expand if people want to buy more units, or shrink if people want to sell back units. An investment trust is an ordinary limited company whose purpose is to invest in securities.

Most stock exchange transactions involve the exchange of existing securities between investors. Only a small proportion of transactions consists of new issues, by companies or by governments. New issues of ordinary shares are a far less important source of funds for most companies than retained profits.

Since investors value liquidity – the ability to sell quickly at close to current prices if they need the money – the existence of **secondary markets** makes it much easier to raise money on the **primary market** than it would otherwise be. Figure 8.1 illustrates the difference between (a) the primary and (b) secondary functions of the stock exchange. In (a) the company is issuing new shares to A, B, C and D and receives the cash. In (b) the company is not directly involved in the transactions and does not receive any cash. Shareholder A is not dealing; B is selling shares to D; and C is selling shares to E, at the market price at the time of each deal. Privatizations were normally type (b): one shareholder (the government) was selling its shares to the public.

The capital invested by companies and by governments is often reflected in fixed physical assets, such as equipment, buildings, roads, and so on. Thus businesses may tend to be 'anchored' to a particular location or type of business. This may also be true to some extent of employees and suppliers. But if a market exists where investors can buy and sell shares in the ownership of these assets, a shareholder possesses wealth which is 'mobile'. He can sell his shares to someone else if he needs the cash for consumption; or if he wants to invest instead in another kind of business or in another country; or if he just loses confidence in a particular company or country.

The presence of short-term **speculators** helps the market. **Bulls** buy shares expecting them to rise (probably in the fairly short term), while **bears** look for prices to fall. They either sell shares they do not even own (**'selling short'**), hoping to buy them later at lower prices; or at least refrain from buying yet, planning to do so more cheaply later. They may also deal in options – though these can be used to *reduce* risk rather than to speculate.

If on balance speculators make profits, that implies that their views are 'more correct' than other people's. Their actions drive market prices *sooner* to levels they would otherwise take longer to reach. (This may also be true of **'insiders'**.) In this way – and without intending it (Adam Smith's 'invisible hand'!) – they help improve the trustworthiness of market prices as signals to investors.

Stock market indices

There is interest in the equity market as a whole, as well as in specific industries and companies. Three main indices show how the equity market is performing.

1. The FT ordinary share index
The 30-share FT ordinary share index contains leading shares from most business sectors. It began as long ago as 1935, though most of the shares comprising it have changed since then. The index shows how leading shares have moved in the short term, from hour to hour. It is a geometric average (taking the 30th root of the product of all the share prices multiplied together), and is not suitable for long-term comparisons.

2. The FT-Actuaries 500-share index
The 500-share index, started in 1962, gives a wide coverage of UK shares. The 500-share index is an arithmetical average, and is suitable for long-term comparisons. Figure 8.2 shows it from 1968 to 1993, adjusted for inflation. The sharp and prolonged 75 per cent fall in 1973 and 1974 is striking: it contrasts with the 25 per cent fall in the 1987 'crash' (which, however, happened almost overnight). The five-year bull market from 1982 to 1987 roughly tripled the real level of equities; but it was only in 1987 that the previous peak of 1972 was breached in real terms. The real level in June 1994 was only about 4 per cent above the 1972 peak in real terms. The FT 500 has recently been renamed FT–SE–A Non-Financials Index.

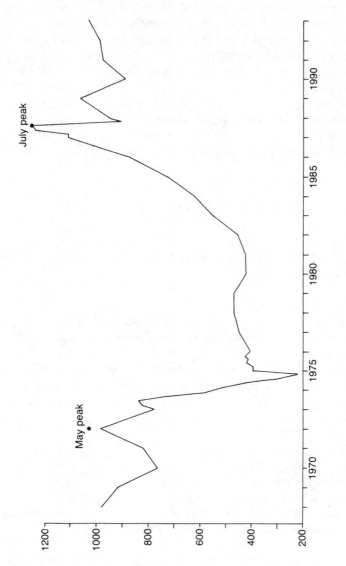

Figure 8.2 FT-Actuaries 500-share index, 1968–93 (in constant January 1987 purchasing power)

Table 8.1 Market capitalization of the largest 10 companies in the FT-SE 100, 2 July 1994 (£bn.)

British Telecom	22.9
Shell Transport	22.7
British Petroleum	21.4
Glaxo	16.5
BTR	12.9
Hanson	12.4
Hong Kong and Shanghai Banking	12.4
BAT Industries	12.3
British Gas	11.5
Marks & Spencer	11.1

3. The FT-SE 100-share index

The FT-SE 100-share index ('Footsie') began in 1984. The Footsie index is calculated minute by minute on the basis of the 100 largest listed companies (in terms of market capitalization). Prices come directly from the Stock Exchange Automated Quotations system (SEAQ). The constituents have changed frequently (at the margin), especially as large utilities have been privatized. Together the 100 constituent companies comprise about two-thirds of the total value of the UK-listed equity market, some £720 billion. Table 8.1 shows the market capitalization of the largest ten UK companies in July 1994.

Issuing equity shares

Going public

A company may wish to list its ordinary shares on the stock exchange for two main reasons: to raise more share capital from the public; or to enable existing shareholders to sell some of their shares. When a company 'goes public' it must issue a **prospectus** naming the directors and giving the company's history, its recent financial results and certain other details.

Normally a company must offer at least 25 per cent of the ordinary shares to the public in order to ensure a free market in the shares. For small companies, the **unlisted securities market** (USM) has less stringent requirements. For example, a USM company need offer only 10 per cent of its shares to the public.

Pricing new shares may be difficult if there are few directly comparable companies. If the price of a new issue (fixed some days in advance) is too high, nobody will buy, and the **underwriters** will have to take up the shares; but if the price is too low, the issuing company's existing shareholders will find their equity interest diluted.

The costs of issuing shares to the public can be high. There would need to be a price discount (of between 10 and 20 per cent) to attract buyers of risky new shares in a little-known company. Moreover underwriting costs, fees to professional advisers, printing and advertising costs, would total at least 5 per cent of the proceeds. And for small companies the amount of management time involved can be significant.

There are three main methods of going public, as follows:

1. An **offer for sale** offers shares to the public at large, at a fixed price. This is a common method for larger issues. The issuing house may itself take up all the shares before selling them on to the public.

2. The issuing house may '**place**' a new issue (below a certain size) privately with its clients, including financial institutions, at a price fixed in advance. A proportion must be made available to market-makers to ensure a market in the shares. There may be lower expenses than for other methods of issue, but a higher market discount.

3. The **tender method** sets no fixed price in advance. Instead it solicits offers from the public; and the highest price which will raise all the required money becomes the asking price for all successful purchases. The market discount is likely to be small, which discourages **stags** (bulls of new issues).

Several of the nationalized enterprises that have been privatized used the offer-for-sale method, and the fixed price was often much less than the level the shares immediately rose to on the market. The general view is that the government sacrificed large sums to ensure the political 'success' of these issues. (On the other hand, sales proceeds may have been increased by privatizing some industries as monopolies (gas) or duopolies (power generation) rather than with a more competitive structure.)

When a company makes some of its equity shares available to the public for the first time, it is often an opportunity both for the company itself to raise some new money and for existing shareholders to sell some of their holdings. Thus the total proceeds of the issue may need to be split between the company and its existing shareholders.

Rights issues

The methods of issue just described apply to unlisted companies going public for the first time. Companies whose shares are already listed normally use a **rights issue** to raise more equity money (over and above equity funds raised by retaining profits and not distributing them in dividends). This is because the stock exchange regards rights issues as being fairest to existing shareholders.

A rights issue offers extra shares to existing shareholders, in proportion to their holdings, priced at some discount from the current market price per share. In theory the price of a rights issue does not matter. An existing shareholder who is unwilling to take up the new shares can (in the UK) always sell his rights in the market and thus avoid any loss from **dilution**. Indeed, if necessary the company will do so on behalf of any shareholders who do not take up their rights. (Of course, the offer price of a rights issue must be below the current market price, otherwise anyone who wants to buy more shares would simply do so in the market, not by way of the rights!)

Example

Thomas Lodge plc has 50 million ordinary shares already in issue, with a current market price of 150p each. The company plans to raise an extra £20 million of equity capital by means of a rights issue. Table 8.2 shows two different ways of achieving this (ignoring transaction costs): either issuing 1 for 1 @ 40p, or else issuing 2 for 5 @ 100p.

Table 8.2 Rights issue: alternative issue prices

	1 for 1 @ 40p	2 for 5 @ 100p
Number of new shares to be issued	50 million	20 million
New total number of shares (n)	100 million	70 million
New share price (£95m/n)	95p	135.71p
Value of the rights per share	55p	35.71p

Table 8.3   Taking up or selling rights (£)

	1 for 1 @ 40p		2 for 5 @ 100p	
	AY	NO	AY	NO
Opening holding @ 150p: 1000 shares	1,500	1,500	1,500	1,500
Buy 1,000 shares @ 40p	400			
Buy 400 shares @ 100p			400	
Sell 1000 rights @ 55p		(550)		
Sell 400 rights @ 35.71p:				(143)
Closing holding @ 95p (135.71p):				
AY: 2,000 (1,400) shares	1,900		1,900	
NO: 1,000 (1,000) shares		950		1,357

Alan Yarrow (AY) owns 1,000 shares and decides to take up his rights in full; while Norman Oliver (NO), who also owns 1,000 shares, decides to sell all his rights. Table 8.3 shows that in each case the market value of AY's holding goes up to reflect the amount of extra cash he has invested; and in each case the market value of NO's holding goes down by exactly the amount of cash he receives for selling his rights.

Bonus issues and share splits

So far we have been discussing two kinds of share issues on the stock exchange: new listings, which usually raise new money for a company, but which may merely transfer shares from existing shareholders to new ones; and rights issues, by which listed companies raise new capital from their existing shareholders (or from those who buy the 'rights' to subscribe).

Two kinds of share issues raise no new money for companies, but can affect the meaning of certain stock exchange ratios as follows:

1. **Bonus issues (scrip issues)** capitalize some of a company's reserves, by transferring them on the balance sheet to called-up share capital. This is purely a bookkeeping entry. The total amount of shareholders' funds remains the same as before, since no new money has been raised; but the company has turned some of its retained profits, or other reserves, into called-up ordinary share capital (so they are no longer available to pay out in dividends).

2. **Share splits** simply 'split' shares into smaller units without even affecting balance sheet amounts.

Example
Giant plc has 600,000 ordinary £1 shares in issue, with a market price of £12 each. After the company makes a '4 for 1' share split, it will have 2.4 million ordinary shares of 25p each in issue each with a market price of 300p. Notice that a '4 for 1' share split means 4 new shares *instead of* each existing share in issue; whereas a '4 for 1' bonus issue means 4 new shares *in addition to* each existing share held, making 5 in all.

In comparing earnings per share (or other 'per share' amounts) over time, it may be necessary to adjust earlier years' figures to allow for subsequent share splits or bonus issues.

What is the purpose of making bonus issues or of splitting shares? They 'give' shareholders nothing they did not already own: they do not increase the total market value of the equity capital. One obvious effect is to reduce the per-share market price on the stock exchange; but there is no reason – either in theory or in practice – to think this matters.

Dividend policy

Do dividends matter?

Ordinary dividends are cash payments by a company out of profits to its shareholders. In a 'perfect' capital market, with no taxes or **transaction costs**, dividend policy would not affect shareholders' wealth. Dividends would transfer cash to shareholders, but the market value of the shares would precisely reflect any retained profits. Any shareholders who wanted more cash than a company paid in dividends could simply sell some of their shares, in effect 'declaring their own dividends'.

Example
To begin with, John Smith owned 25 per cent of the shares in two identical companies, Adam plc and Bede plc. Adam paid out all its profits each year in dividends, whereas Bede retained all its profits to reinvest. Smith kept his 25 per cent shareholding in Adam,

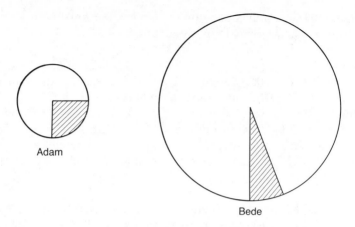

Figure 8.3   Smith's shareholdings in Adam and Bede after some years

which (with no retained profits) stayed the same size. Each year Smith sold enough shares in Bede, which (by retaining all its profits) was growing larger, to provide the same amount of cash as Adam's dividends.

After some years, Bede was much larger than Adam, but Smith's reducing share in Bede was worth exactly the same as his constant 25 per cent share in Adam. Since Smith had also received the same amount of cash from his shareholding in each company (either in dividends or from the sale of some shares), the companies' different dividend policies had (in theory) had exactly the same effect on Smith's wealth. (In this presumed perfect market there were no taxes or transaction costs.) Figure 8.3 shows the position.

In the real world the tax position of shareholders can vary, from tax exempt pension funds to higher-rate taxpayers. So it can be hard for companies to tell what dividend policy might be best for 'shareholders as a whole'. Transaction costs, too, matter in practice. A company which paid out 'too much' dividend one year would certainly find it very expensive to make a rights issue (a 'negative dividend'!) the next year to compensate.

Taxes on shareholders' returns

A company aiming to maximize its shareholders' wealth (see Chapter 1) needs to take account of income tax on dividends and

capital gains tax. Pension funds and insurance companies (see Chapter 1) are liable to neither: they are called **'gross funds'**. Individual shareholders' marginal tax rate on dividends may be zero, 20 per cent, or 40 per cent if their taxable income exceeds £23,700 per year.

From 1993, companies deduct advance corporation tax (ACT) from dividends at 20 per cent (no longer at the basic rate of 25 per cent). They pay the ACT to the Inland Revenue soon after paying the net dividend to shareholders. Thus a net dividend of £300 represents a 'gross' dividend of £375, less ACT of 20 per cent (= £75). Gross funds can reclaim the 20 per cent, and basic rate taxpayers need pay no more tax. But higher-rate taxpayers will be liable to extra income tax of 20 per cent on the gross dividends (making 40 per cent in all). The gross funds are also exempt from capital gains tax, and most small shareholders are unlikely to pay any. But capital gains tax may be payable both by companies and by some higher-rate shareholders. Taxable capital gains bear the same marginal tax rate as dividend income, but tax-paying shareholders may still prefer capital gains to dividends. They are indexed for inflation, capital losses are offsettable, £5,800 of real gains are exempt each year, and there is a delay in making the capital gains tax payment.

From a company's viewpoint, ACT on dividends (as the name implies) represents an advance payment of corporation tax. The balance – **'mainstream' corporation tax** – is normally payable nine months after the company's financial year-end. But a company without enough taxable UK profits will have **unrecovered ACT**, which it may carry forward to set off in future. If there is little prospect of this, then the prudence concept will lead accounts to write it off as an extra expense ('irrecoverable ACT').

Why might UK companies not have enough UK taxable profits? They might be making losses, and paying dividends out of past retentions; or large writing-down allowances might mean they have no taxable profits; or their profits might come mainly from outside the UK. To deal with this latter problem the 1994 Finance Act contains some thirty pages of complex legislation on 'Foreign Income Dividends' (out of over 400 pages in total!).

Choosing a policy

Most listed UK companies pay an **interim** and a **final dividend** each year, with the final dividend usually being larger. (This contrasts with the American practice of equal quarterly dividends.) At an annual general meeting, shareholders may vote to *reduce* the amount of a proposed final dividend, but they cannot increase it. (Thus, rather strangely, they can vote to increase, but not to reduce, the amount of retained earnings for a period.)

Should a company first decide on a dividend, and then regard any profits left over (retained profits) as available for investment? Or should it first choose how much to reinvest, and then treat dividends as the residual? Most companies seem to do the former, basing the current year's dividend on last year's payout. Dividends normally increase from year to year, both to keep pace with inflation, and to reflect increased real earnings (which become more likely the higher the amount of retained earnings).

Retained profits have been the most important source of funds for most UK companies. But historical money cost accounts, which overstate 'real' profits, overstate 'real' *retained* profits too! This may help explain why 1994 stockmarket levels are hardly above 1972 levels despite 22 years of apparent (often large) retained profits (see Chapter 8). Where companies treat dividends almost as fixed amounts, retained profits for a period can fluctuate more sharply than earnings. Where there are losses, of course, retained profits for the period (not the cumulative total) will be negative. This will also be true where dividends paid exceed profits for a period.

If retained profits represent a volatile source of funds, how can managers respond? They can reduce the amount of new investment, sell some existing assets for cash, borrow, or issue more equity capital. Without very good reason, most companies are reluctant either to increase gearing much, or to issue more equity shares. If there are no obvious surplus assets to sell, therefore, they may try to keep dividends down to a level where they can expect to finance new investment projects out of retained profits (plus depreciation).

We can value company shares on the basis of future dividends (see Chapter 10), but ultimately it is earnings that matter. Where companies try to keep their **dividend payout ratio** (or its reciprocal, the **dividend cover**) fairly constant, dividends per share will grow at much the same rate as earnings.

Companies with few profitable investment opportunities may tend to pay out a high proportion of their after-tax profits in dividends; while companies with many projects to invest in may prefer a lower payout ratio. But this might be a medium-term policy; it need not imply a constant payout ratio every year.

For most companies the dividend payout tends to follow the 'step-like' pattern of Figure 8.4(a), rather than closely following

Pence
per share

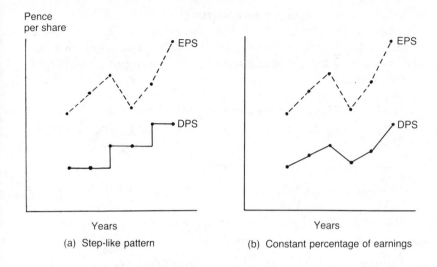

Years	Years
(a) Step-like pattern	(b) Constant percentage of earnings

Figure 8.4 Two patterns of dividend pay-out

earnings from year to year, as in Figure 8.4(b). This will be even more likely in future, with earnings per share under the FRS 3 accounting standard likely to be far more volatile than when 'extraordinary' items could be excluded (under SSAP 6). Now FRS 3 includes them as 'exceptional'.

A loss-making company might not choose to omit its dividend, or even necessarily to reduce it from the previous year's level. For dividend policy can be an important way for management to *communicate* to shareholders about future prospects. The stock market would probably take the maintenance of the dividend by a loss-making company as a signal that earnings would soon recover. In contrast, cutting the dividend could signify that the decline in earnings might take some time to reverse.

Given that in theory dividend policy should not matter, and that it is hard for a company to satisfy all its shareholders if they have widely different marginal tax rates, what can one suggest? Probably the best dividend policy is to follow two general rules. First, tell shareholders clearly what a company's dividend policy actually *is* (rather than letting them try to guess it). Second, try not to change the policy without warning.

Own share purchase

Since 1982 UK companies have been able to buy back their own fully paid ordinary shares. Possible reasons for wanting to do so include the following:

1. Buying out the estates of deceased shareholders.
2. Buying back employee scheme shares when the employee leaves.
3. Buying out dissident shareholders.
4. Offering investors an option to sell their shares back after a time.
5. Reducing capital, possibly to increase financial gearing.
6. Supporting the market for the shares.
7. Converting public companies back into private ones.

Only the last three reasons would be likely to apply to public companies.

The aggregate effect of own-share purchases is similar to dividend payments, in that the company reduces both cash and shareholders' funds. The main difference is that dividends are recurring payments out of profits, whereas own-share purchases tend to be one-off.

For private companies, the purchase price will normally be subject to capital gains tax in shareholders' hands, rather than **income tax**. Only real capital gains will be taxable, and even if the marginal tax rates are the same, capital gains tax will normally be payable later.

Section 162 of the Companies Act 1985 contains the legal rules. Companies which buy back their own shares must *cancel* them, not hold them 'in treasury' available for reissue, as in the United States. The company's Articles must authorize purchase of own shares on the market; and an ordinary resolution must specify the maximum number of shares, and a date within eighteen months when the power to purchase will expire.

In order to maintain a company's capital, the purchase monies must normally come either from distributable profits or from the proceeds of a fresh issue of shares for the purpose. Also the company must transfer certain amounts to a 'capital redemption reserve'. But where its Articles expressly permit it, a *private* company may purchase its own shares out of *capital*.

9

Valuing equity

Modern portfolio theory

Shareholder diversification

Modern portfolio theory (MPT) holds that investment involves two different kinds of risk: **market risk** and **unique risk**. Equity investors cannot avoid market risk, which stems from the uncertainties of the whole economy. In contrast, unique risk relates to a particular company or a specific project. Shareholders can, in effect, avoid it by investing in several different kinds of projects (or shares).

An investor who splits his equity equally among a dozen different shares (of companies in different industries) can **diversify** away more than half the total risk he would bear by investing everything in a single equity share. In effect, a portfolio 'averages out' the unique risks of the different shares. But he *cannot* diversify away about one-third of the total risk of a single security however many shares he holds. It represents the residual risk to which all shares (and projects) are subject. As Figure 9.1 shows, increasing the number of holdings beyond about a dozen equity investments makes little further difference in reducing unique risk.

This points to an important difference of outlook between managers of a company and its shareholders. Managers (like workers) are often committed largely to a particular company, and may therefore be concerned with its *total* risk (that is, both market risk and unique risk). Shareholders, on the other hand, are 'mobile' (see Chapter 8),

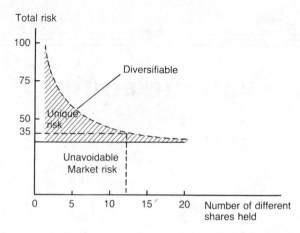

Figure 9.1   Unique risk and market risk

and presumably hold diversified portfolios. So the theory says they need care only about market risk. One important question is the extent to which market pressures force managers to act in the interests of shareholders (by worrying only about market risk, as opposed to total risk).

This theory concerning risk, and how the market values assets (it is often referred to as the **capital asset pricing model** – or simply **CAPM**), also has implications with respect to profit-seeking. Is it really, as the theory implies, more rational for shareholders to hold diversified portfolios, in order to avoid risks for which they cannot expect to receive any reward? Or is it, as some successful investors in the past have believed, better to 'put all one's eggs in one basket – and then *watch the basket closely*?

Market risk

Modern portfolio theory says that no investor *needs* to take on unique risks: he can get rid of them by holding shares in several *different* companies. Hence market returns will compensate only for 'market risk'. Unfortunately these two kinds of risk have several different names each, as listed in Table 9.1.

The theory says that the required return on any particular share bears a definite relationship (known as **beta**) to the return on an investment in the 'market' as a whole ('return' means dividend plus capital gain). An investment with a beta of less than 1.0 is less 'risky'

Table 9.1 Synonyms for two different kinds of risk

Market risk	Unique risk
Non-diversifiable risk	Diversifiable risk
Systematic risk	Unsystematic risk
	Specific risk

than the whole market; with a beta of more than 1.0, more risky. (In this context, 'risk' means the volatility of a share's returns.) Figure 9.2 shows the spread of betas for companies in the FT-SE 100-share index. It is not easy, even for listed companies, to translate the company's beta into a beta for a particular project.

To find the *required* after-tax rate of return for a particular investment, simply add a risk premium to the after-tax risk-free rate of return. In MPT this risk premium is the whole market's required after-tax risk premium multiplied by the particular investment's beta. Based on actual past results over many decades (similar in the United Kingdom and the United States), an investment in the equity stock market as a whole requires a real after-tax risk premium of about 8 per cent a year on top of the 'risk-free' rate of return on government securities.

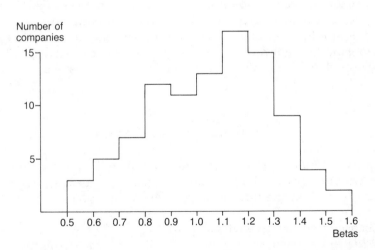

Figure 9.2 Betas for the companies in the FT-SE 100-share index, June 1993 (Source: London Business School Risk Measurement Service)

Table 9.2 Required rates of return for Project E and Project F

Project	Required after-tax risk-free return		Estimated beta		Required market risk premium		Required project risk premium		Required project rate of return
E	5%	+	(0.75	×	8%	=)	6%	=	11%
F	5%	+	(1.5	×	8%	=)	12%	=	17%

Example

Project E (which might be an ordinary share in Company E), with an estimated beta of 0.75, will have a risk premium of 6.0 per cent; while Project F, with a beta of 1.5, will have a risk premium of 12.0 per cent. Assuming the required risk-free after-tax money return is 5.0 per cent, the required project rates of return (or 'cost of equity capital') will be 11 per cent and 17 per cent respectively, as set out in Table 9.2.

Figure 9.3 shows the capital market line with a straight-line relationship between market risk (β) and required rate of return. It starts from the after-tax 'risk-free rate of return' (assumed to be 5 per cent), and adds a 'risk premium' – the 'market' risk premium of 8 per cent multiplied by the project's own beta. (Both these numbers are only estimates.) The beta refers *only* to 'market risk'. It ignores a project's 'unique risk' (also called '**specific risk**') on the grounds that any investor can avoid it by holding a diversified portfolio.

If Project E has an expected return of 12 per cent, and if Project F has an expected return of 16 per cent, then Project E is acceptable, but Project F (which is higher-return but also higher-risk) is not.

Problems with CAPM

The CAPM formula for the cost of equity capital is $R_f + \beta (R_m - R_f)$. In interpreting the meaning of this formula, a number of problems arise. We can take the three main components in order.

R_f, the required risk-free rate of return

1. What time period is appropriate? Is it very short-term govern-ment securities, such as 90-day Treasury Bills? Or should we be matching the maturity with the life of the project, say, fifteen

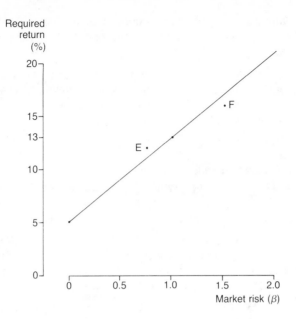

Figure 9.3 The capital market line

years? (The answer may depend on consistency with the definition of 'R$_f$' used in the expression (R$_m$ − R$_f$).)

2. Presumably if we want the money cost of equity capital, we shall need to use a money risk-free rate. But can we take the yield on index-linked gilts as equivalent to the risk-free *real* rate? Or is it really (as BZW argue) somewhat less than that?

3. What about tax? Should we assume the equity investor is a tax-free financial institution? Or a basic rate taxpayer (20 or 25 per cent)? Or a higher-rate taxpayer? Should we assume that tax rates will stay the same in future? (Because the majority of shares in listed companies are held by tax-free institutions, it may be better to ignore personal income tax.)

β, the relationship to market risk

4. Is it true (as Van Horne suggests) that company betas vary 'considerably' depending which version of the 'stock market' you use? And how unstable are company betas over time? Why is a sixty-month past period appropriate in calculating a company's beta, rather than six months or sixty years?

5. How can we translate the estimated beta of a listed company into a suitable beta for an unlisted company? Or for a particular project?

6. Should we use a (geared) equity beta (which is what the published numbers usually are), or an (ungeared) asset beta? The former relates to the cost of equity capital, the latter to an average cost of (debt plus equity) capital.

$(R_m - R_f)$, the market risk premium

7. Is it acceptable to use simply the domestic stock market as a basis for calculating the required 'market' risk premium? Or should we take a wider basis, covering international markets too, or using a much wider set of assets?

8. Over what time period should the market risk premium be calculated? The last five years or the last fifty years? In any case, are we entitled to assume that the future will be like the past?

9. Is the market risk premium of about 8 per cent a year (which is in real terms) before tax or (as is normally assumed) after tax? How can we allow for a changing tax system over time? Is there any significant difference between US and UK conditions?

General

10. Are we really indifferent to unique risk? What about (a) managers and (b) family businesses who are *not* fully diversified?

11. Most betas of listed companies seem to be between 0.7 and 1.3 (that is, fairly close to 1.0). Is all the fuss really worth it?

12. Given that many aspects of investment are likely to be more important than refining the supposed 'accuracy' of the discount rate, might it make sense to limit one's use of CAPM to estimating whether the *industry* concerned seems to be low, average, or high risk? Then one could similarly distinguish between cost reduction, expansion, and new product projects (as respectively low risk, average risk, and high risk).

The point of the above questions is not to denigrate the Capital Asset Pricing Model. But it would be absurd to pretend its results can be precisely accurate in practice. Too many questionable assumptions have to be made.

Other share valuation methods

The dividend growth model

In principle we can value equity shares in the same way as risk-free securities (see Chapter 8). Thus we discount the expected future cash receipts from owning the shares, using the opportunity cost of capital. Instead of a regular fixed money **annuity**, we now have to deal with dividends which can fluctuate. A common simplifying assumption is that, in money terms, the latest annual net dividend per share will grow at a *constant* rate in future.

Dividend payments do *not* represent the whole cost of equity capital. Equity capital still has an 'opportunity cost' even for a company which pays no dividends: it is what the shareholders could otherwise have done with the money invested. Hence it is the discounting rate that shareholders (presumably) apply to the expected future dividends. A shareholder's 'return' from holding shares consists of two parts: dividends plus **capital gain** (or less capital loss). Yet the stock market can value a company's equity shares *solely* on the basis of expected future cash dividends.

It is true that an individual mortal shareholder (A) (or his estate) will ultimately sell his shares. But he will sell to some other shareholder (B), who will value the shares on the basis of future dividends plus ultimate sales proceeds. Table 9.3 shows how we can 'cancel out' the various intermediate purchases and sales, ending up with valuing the shares only on the basis of the stream of future

Table 9.3 Valuing shares solely on the basis of future dividends

Shareholder	Cost of purchase	Cash receipts from holding shares	
		Dividends	Sales proceeds
A	Value EOY 0	= Dividends EOY 1–10 +	Value EOY 10
B	Value EOY 10	= Dividends EOY 11–20 +	Value EOY 20
C	Value EOY 20	= Dividends EOY 21–30 +	Value EOY 30
D	Value EOY 30	= Dividends EOY 31–40 +	Value EOY 40
E	Value EOY 40	= . . .	
. . .			
	Value EOY 0	= Dividends EOY 1–40 . . .	

dividends. For simplicity we assume that shareholders A, B, C, D, etc. hold the shares for exactly ten years each. Clearly we could pursue the logic right through the alphabet.

Applying the present value model to share valuation is straight-forward enough in theory, though of course in practice guessing the actual numbers is not easy.

If the latest annual net dividend per share is d, the expected (assumed constant) rate of growth in future net dividends per share is g, and the opportunity cost of equivalent-risk equity shares is k, then we find the present value per share (p) by discounting the expected future dividends *for ever*, as follows:

$$p = \frac{d(1+g)}{(1+k)} + \frac{d(1+g)^2}{(1+k)^2} + \frac{d(1+g)^3}{(1+k)^3} + \ldots + \frac{d(1+g)^\infty}{(1+k)^\infty}$$

This can be simplified* to:

$$p = \frac{d^1}{k-g}$$

or

$$k = \frac{d^1}{p} + g$$

In words: the cost of equity capital (k) is the expected current-year net dividend yield (d'/p) plus the annual (assumed constant) rate of

---

* Multiply both sides of the equation shown by $\dfrac{(1+k)}{(1+g)}$

Then from the resulting product, subtract the equation shown above. This gives

$$p\frac{(1+k)}{(1+g)} - p = d^0 - d\frac{(1+g)^\infty}{(1+k)^\infty}$$

Since $k > g$, the final term collapses to zero, which leaves:

$$p\frac{(1+k)}{(1+g)} - p = d^0$$

leading to $p(1+k) - p(1+g) = d^0(1+g)$

hence $p(k-g) = d^1$

growth (g) in net dividends per share. Because shareholders may have different tax positions, estimating the 'after-tax' amount of dividends can be difficult. But in practice guessing the value of g normally matters more than correctly adjusting for tax on d.

Example
Burnham Ltd is expected to pay a net dividend this year on ordinary shares of 11p; the expected future growth rate in dividends per share is 10 per cent a year; and the opportunity cost of equity capital is reckoned to be 15 per cent a year. Using the dividend growth model, Burnham Ltd's ordinary shares would be valued at 220p each.

$$\text{Value} = \frac{11}{0.15 - 0.10} = \frac{11}{0.05} = 220\text{p}$$

To determine the opportunity cost of equity capital we simply add the assumed constant growth rate (of 10 per cent a year in this case) to the net dividend yield (of 5 per cent a year), based on d' – the end-of-current-year dividend. In this case this gives an (after-tax) cost of equity capital of 15 per cent a year. Both k and g are only rough estimates, so the difference between them ($k - g$) may be subject to a very large margin of error.

Price/earnings multiple

When we already know the market price per share (for a listed company), we can divide it by the latest **earnings per share** to calculate the **price/earnings ratio** (or multiple). Its reciprocal, the earnings per share divided by the market price, is called the 'earnings yield'. But for an unquoted company (Snibbo Ltd) we might know the earnings (profit after tax), and want to estimate the value – either per share or for the whole company.

We might take the current price/earnings ratio for a listed company in the same industry, and reduce it slightly to allow for Snibbo's extra risks (being smaller and unquoted). We could then multiply Snibbo's earnings by the adjusted price/earnings ratio, to estimate the value.

Clearly a higher price/earnings ratio means a higher market value for any given level of earnings (and current dividend). It implies either a faster growth rate in future dividends (g in our formula), or else a lower cost of capital (k). But this is fair enough: if we value returns and dislike risk, then we would expect a higher value for a company with either higher expected returns or lower perceived risks than another.

The price/earnings ratio does not represent literally the 'number of years' future earnings' included in the price. The discounting process means that future earnings are worth less than the same amount of earnings this year. Thus a price/earnings ratio of 9, for example, does *not* mean that we are looking only nine years ahead: as we know, in principle our valuation formula includes estimated future dividends *for ever*. (Nothing 'short-termist' about that!)

Book value

Another method simply assumes a company's equity to be 'worth' the **book value** of equity (shareholders' funds) in the latest balance sheet. This is not really adequate, since **historical cost** balance sheets merely show the original cost of some assets, less amounts written off. They do not pretend to show **current values** especially for fixed assets; and even if they did, current value balance sheets may still leave out many assets (especially intangible ones).

Nevertheless, for unquoted companies, partnerships and sole traders, book values are at least *available*; and despite their serious drawbacks, they are quite often used in practice as a starting point for valuing firms. In particular, the book values of current assets may be quite close to their current value; it is likely to be the fixed assets that are much harder to value.

Liquidation value

Liquidation (or break-up) value is the minimum value of assets of a business. If expected future cash earnings have a present value less than the assets could be sold for, then the business should sell the assets now. We would value the company at the total net realizable value of its separate assets (less creditors), whatever their balance sheet **net book values**.

Whoever buys the assets must be planning to earn future cash flows from them, which he presumably expects to produce a present value higher than the purchase price. The buyer thinks he can use the assets more profitably or less riskily than the seller thinks he (the seller) can. Their different subjective valuations of the assets are what makes a deal possible.

Why share prices fluctuate

There can be three kinds of reason why a share's price may fluctuate, as follows:

1. There may be a change to the current year's net dividend (d'). Clearly a change that the market has already anticipated will not affect the share price: only unanticipated changes will do so. This is one reason why the share price sometimes goes up when a company announces bad news: the market may have been expecting even worse.

2. The expected future growth rate in net dividends per share (g) may vary, perhaps more or less in line with expected future growth in *earnings* per share (which would imply a more or less constant dividend cover). There are many possible reasons for future earnings to vary: new management, technological inventions, competitive activity, changes in customer tastes, new government policies, and so on.

3. A change in the 'opportunity cost of capital' (k) could also cause the share price to vary. There are many reasons why the market's view of the riskiness of a particular company's equity shares might alter. An analysis of all the reasons might start by distinguishing between 'business risk' and 'financial risk'.

Thus any change in the future prospects of a business – especially its future earnings or the risk involved – may affect a share's present market value. Since life is uncertain, with new information, new conditions, and new perceptions of the future ever emerging, it is hardly surprising that share prices continually fluctuate. Only in an unchanging world where everything in the future had already been fully and correctly foreseen would this not be so.

10

Corporate finance

Cost of capital

Overall cost of capital

A firm's **cost of capital** is 'that rate of return which its assets must produce in order to justify raising the funds to acquire them'. We have discussed briefly how to calculate a company's after-tax cost of debt capital (Chapter 8) and its cost of equity capital (Chapter 9). Combining them gives the company's overall **weighted average cost of capital (WACC)**. This is the basis for a discount rate to use in assessing capital investment projects.

Example
If a company has equity capital with a market value of £12 million, and debt capital with a market value of £4 million, weights of ¾ and ¼ respectively apply to the cost of equity and the cost of debt. Using costs of 15 per cent for equity and 6 per cent for debt, the result is an overall cost of capital of 12¾ per cent: (¾ × 15) + (¼ × 6). In practice we would round this up and use 13 per cent for the WACC.

Figure 10.1 shows that the overall weighted average cost of capital is not very sensitive to the weights of debt and equity. As the debt ratio increases from 10 per cent to 50 per cent (almost the whole range within which most companies' debt ratios fall), the WACC falls only from 14.1 per cent to 10.5 per cent. For the same reason, it

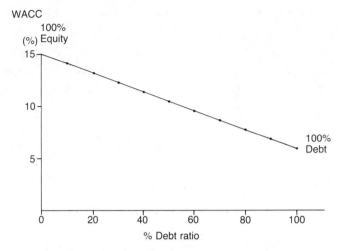

Figure 10.1   How WACC varies with changing debt ratios

usually does not matter too much whether the weights are based on market values or book values. (As debt ratio increases, one would expect the cost of debt – and probably of equity too – to increase. The effect would be to increase WACC, and thus further reduce its decline over the whole range of debt ratios.)

As a rule business people *separate* two questions: (a) whether a project is worth investing in or not; and (b) if so, how to finance it. Even if a company plans to finance a particular project by borrowing, therefore, it still bases the required rate of return on the overall average cost of capital. (Notice that the WACC is a weighted average of *marginal* costs!) Otherwise a 'worse' project to be financed by debt might (wrongly) be preferred to a 'better' project to be financed by equity.

Nearly all the numbers are only *estimates*: the amounts and the timing of the future cash flows from a capital project, the cost of debt, and the cost of equity. For this reason, it is probably not worth distinguishing between two kinds of equity capital, even though share issues would involve some extra costs, and therefore be somewhat more expensive than retained profits.

Adjusting WACC for risk

Rather than using WACC itself as the hurdle rate for all capital projects (the horizontal line in Figure 10.2), a company may choose

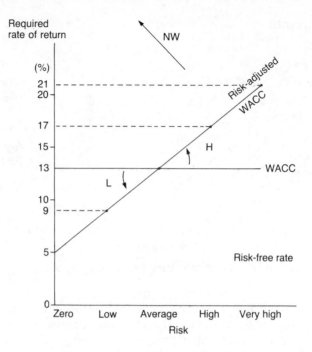

Figure 10.2   Adjusting WACC for risk

to adjust the WACC upwards (= 'require a higher rate of return') for 'high-risk' projects, and to adjust the WACC downwards for 'low-risk' projects. Otherwise there would be a tendency to accept too many high-risk projects (such as H), and to reject too many low-risk projects (such as L).

How much to adjust WACC for risk is a matter of judgement. The cash flows for capital projects are usually based on such fallible estimates that a difference of one or two percentage points in the discount rate is unlikely to be critical.

For a project with zero risk, the appropriate required rate of return would be the (after-tax) risk-free rate of return – say, 5 per cent. (*Not* 0 per cent, of course!) The WACC itself, say, 13 per cent, would be a suitable required rate of return for a 'typical' project with 'average' risk.

A rough rule of thumb for other projects might be as follows: for a project thought to have below-average risk, move halfway from 'average' to 'zero' risk (that is, to a required rate of return of 9 per cent – halfway between 13 per cent and 5 per cent); for a project with an above-average level of risk, move as much above the WACC (to 17 per cent); and for a very high-risk project, move as far again above WACC (to 21 per cent).

Of course, managers are not merely trying to measure levels of risk and required return. They are also trying to manage the projects in order to 'move' them to the 'north-west' (on Figure 10.2) – either to the 'west' (by reducing the risk), or to the 'north' (by increasing the return), or both.

We saw earlier (Chapter 7) how lenders may seek to reduce their risk (by personal guarantees, by taking security, or by loan covenants). Similarly business managers may seek to reduce risk by various means, such as: extensive market research; arranging long-term sales contracts; or dual sourcing (see Figure 6.10). Managers may also try to increase returns, for example by: expanding the volume of sales; increasing selling prices; or reducing costs without hurting quality. (These may be easier to say than to do!)

De-gearing betas

In calculating the weighted average cost of capital (WACC), we average the cost of equity and the cost of debt. For this purpose we may use a cost of equity capital based either on the capital asset pricing model (CAPM) or on the dividend growth model (see Chapter 9).

Another way of reaching a similar result is to use the capital asset pricing model, but with an **'asset beta'** reflecting only the company's 'business risk', rather than an **'equity beta'** (which we have been using so far), which reflects both **business risk** and **financial risk** (gearing). For example, suppose a company has an equity beta of 1.4, debt represents 25 per cent of the total capital, and (to simplify) the cost of debt is the same as the risk-free rate of return, namely 5 per cent. Then the cost of equity capital will be 16.2 per cent: 5 per cent + 1.4(8); and the weighted average cost of capital will be 13.4 per cent: $(\frac{3}{4} \times 16.2) + (\frac{1}{4} \times 5.0)$.

Another way to calculate the same WACC is as follows. The 'overall' asset beta should be a weighted average of the debt beta and the equity beta. In this case (to simplify) we are assuming a debt beta of zero. So the expression:

$\frac{1}{4}$(debt beta) + $\frac{3}{4}$(equity beta) = asset beta

simplifies to:

zero + $(\frac{3}{4} \times 1.4)$ = 1.05

Now if the asset beta is 1.05, the appropriate 'average' required rate of return is 13.4 per cent: 5.0 + 1.05(8). The same as before.

In practice, the asset beta would be somewhat higher than this, since the debt beta would be somewhat above zero.

Gearing

How financial gearing works

Financial gearing means borrowing to finance the business, rather than using only equity capital. If the rate of return on assets financed by debt exceeds the cost of borrowing, the extra profit increases equity earnings. Conversely, debt interest must be paid, even if the company's rate of return on assets is lower than the rate of interest on borrowing. When operating profit is high, **gearing** will benefit shareholders, and vice versa.

Example

Brown Ltd and Green Ltd are similar except for their gearing. Total capital employed is £10 million. Brown's debt ratio is 10 per cent, Green's is 50 per cent. The rate of debt interest payable is 10 per cent a year. In Year 1, the before-tax return on capital employed is 30 per cent, in Year 2 only 5 per cent. As a result, as Table 10.1 shows, in Year 1 the return on equity for high-geared Green (37.5 per cent) is much higher than for low-geared Brown (24.2 per cent); whereas in

Table 10.1   Brown and Green: return on equity in Years 1 and 2 (£'000)

	Year 1		Year 2	
	Brown	Green	Brown	Green
Profit before interest and tax	3,000	3,000	500	500
Debt interest (@ 10%)	100	500	100	500
Profit before tax	2,900	2,500	400	0
Tax (@ 25%)	725	625	100	0
Profit after tax	2,175	1,875	300	0
Return on equity (%)	24.2	37.5	3.3	0
Interest cover (times)	30	6	5	1

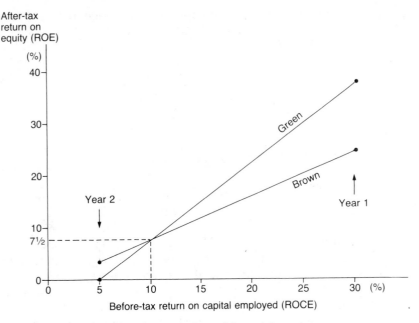

Figure 10.3 The effect of financial gearing

Year 2 the return on equity for low-geared Brown (3.3 per cent) is better than for high-geared Green (0 per cent).

We have looked at only two years' results, but Figure 10.3 plots after-tax return on equity (on the vertical axis) against any rate of before-tax return on capital employed (on the horizontal axis). The after-tax return on equity is the same for both companies at 7½ per cent. This is what we would expect: the 10 per cent rate of debt interest, less the tax rate of 25 per cent.

Gearing and market value

Debt is normally cheaper than equity, partly because it is lower-risk to the investor (see Chapter 7), and partly because interest is normally tax-deductible. So using debt instead of equity should reduce a company's overall cost of capital (WACC). This would reduce the discount rate applying to future cash flows, which means increasing the overall present market value.

If there is 'too much' debt, however, then the extra risks will increase the cost of both debt and equity, until finally the firm's market value will begin to fall (the WACC will begin to increase).

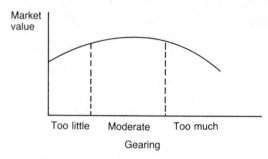

Figure 10.4 Gearing and market value

There is no convincing theory to explain at what level of gearing there is 'too much' debt. A company with high 'business risk' (such as exploring for oil) might not be able to bear much financial risk (gearing) on top; whereas a 'safe' company with low business risk (such as some food companies) might be able to take on quite high levels of gearing without increasing total debt unacceptably.

The 'traditional' view of gearing (Figure 10.4) is that there is an 'optimal range' of capital structure. Over a wide range of moderate gearing, the overall cost of capital is almost flat; and a firm's market value is not very sensitive to minor changes in gearing. Outside the range, however, a company may have too much debt or too little. It can then increase its overall market value (equity plus debt capital) by adjusting its financial gearing (see below), and moving towards the 'optimal range'.

Another approach is the 'pecking order' theory. According to this view, companies do not have any particular 'optimum' or 'target' debt ratio in mind. Instead when they need money to invest in profitable projects, managers prefer retained earnings to debt, and debt to new issues of equity. (Shareholders might prefer debt to retained earnings; but at present cannot give effect to this preference by voting to increase dividends.) Thus companies in the same industry may end up with very different debt ratios simply as a result of historical accident.

Capital structure

Risk and return

Borrowing often appears cheaper after-tax than equity capital; but the *risk* to the borrowing company is higher.

Table 10.2 Rutherfords Ltd: earnings per share calculations (£m.)

	Now	With increased capital		Break-even level	
		Equity	Debt	Equity	Debt
PBIT	15	19	19	11	11
Debt interest	3	3	5	3	5
Profit before tax	12	16	14	8	6
Tax (at 25%)	3	4	3½	2	1½
Profit after tax	9	12	10½	6	4½
Number of ordinary shares (m.)	30	40	30	40	30
EPS (pence)	30	30	35	15	15

Example

Rutherfords Ltd's current level of profit before interest and tax (PBIT) is £15 million a year; current debt interest payable is £3 million a year; and 30 million ordinary shares are outstanding. The company needs £20 million of new capital to finance investment projects which it expects to increase profits (before interest and tax) by £4 million a year.

The choice is between (a) issuing 10 million ordinary shares at 200p net (compared with the current market price of 240p per share), or (b) borrowing £20 million ten-year debentures at 10 per cent a year interest. Should Rutherfords choose debt or equity? On what basis should the company decide?

As a start, we can calculate what earnings per share (EPS) would amount to under each alternative. Table 10.2 shows that if PBIT really does increase by £4 million, the new EPS would stay at 30p if Rutherfords issues 10 million equity shares, and rise to 35p if the company borrows £20 million.

We can also see what is the 'break-even' PBIT level (£x) at which EPS (in the first year) would be the same under the two methods of finance. For Rutherfords, simple algebra shows that the break-even point comes at a PBIT level of £11 million:

$$(\text{Debt})\ \frac{75\%(x-5)}{30} = \frac{75\%(x-3)}{40}\ (\text{Equity})$$

$$40(x-5) = 30(x-3)$$

$$10x = 110$$

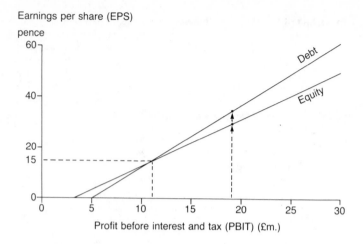

Figure 10.5   Rutherfords Ltd: EPS breakeven chart

Figure 10.5 shows that above the breakeven level of £11 million PBIT, EPS will be higher with debt (due to the effect of gearing); whereas below it, EPS will be higher with the equity issue. (Notice at what PBIT level in each case EPS is zero: £5 million for debt and £3 million for equity.)

We are not entitled to assume that the market value of each ordinary share would necessarily be higher if Rutherfords goes for debt, merely because the EPS would (probably) be higher. That would imply the same price/earnings multiple if the company borrows as if it issues new equity shares. But debt, being riskier for the company, might result in a lower price/earnings multiple than the equity issue.

Just how risky is it for Rutherfords to borrow another £20 million? It would increase the debt ratio from about 30 per cent to about 40 per cent (based on market values); and it would reduce interest cover from 5 times to less than 4 times. In both respects that would seem to be getting towards the maximum comfortable level of debt. (You may wish to see if you can check where these numbers come from.)

The main problem, however, is not to calculate the numbers (on certain assumptions). It is using commercial judgement to balance risks and returns. For example, how likely is PBIT in future to fall below the breakeven level of £11 million? How much would it matter if that did occasionally happen? What might be the impact of future inflation? What effect, if any, might the increased risk from higher borrowing have on the price/earnings multiple (which is currently 8 times)?

Other relevant factors

Choosing about long-term finance is not solely a matter of calculation. Many of the estimates can only be approximate. Moreover other aspects of long-term finance, which are hard to quantify, may be of paramount importance.

Term
The choice between short-term and long-term borrowing depends mainly on comparing the relative costs and risks. To avoid uncertainties, a firm might try to 'match' the period of its borrowing to the period for which it needed the money. Thus it would finance long-term needs (say for a new plant expected to last fifteen years) by long-term money, and short-term needs (say to finance temporarily high raw material stocks) by short-term sources. As a rule one might expect longer-term money to have a higher cost (see Chapter 2).

But a company may not be sure how much money it requires, nor for how long. Estimates of the amount and timing of capital projects can be subject to wide margins of error. It may often make sense to think of a company's needs as consisting of a long-term 'base load' which it can forecast with fair certainty, and a varying balance of short-term needs depending on the nature of the business (see Chapter 4).

Control
For small and medium-sized companies, the question of control of the equity capital is often overriding. The current controlling shareholders are often members of one or two families. They may have limited surplus funds outside the business. Hence they may not want a rights issue of new shares which would dilute their own equity interests and could mean losing control. 'Control' may also refer to certain borrowing arrangements involving covenants or other restrictions (see Chapter 7) which owner/managers may think unacceptable. As a result, some companies may prefer to restrict their possible rate of expansion, even if that means shareholders going without large potential profits.

Flexibility

Even in larger companies (where no small group may own a significant interest in the equity capital), managers will usually value flexibility – keeping their options open (see also Chapter 6). Thus they may choose not to borrow all the way up to some supposed 'optimum' level of gearing if that would rule out any more borrowing for a number of years, or if it would make debt too expensive in time of emergency.

Making a loss, of course, reduces a company's accumulated retained profits and thus the amount of its balance sheet equity. (Paying dividends has the same result.) A seemingly adequate debt ratio can soon become uncomfortably high through one or two years' losses, combined with further borrowing in order to finance current operations. So it is perhaps not surprising if managers sometimes seem (to the outsider) to be rather cautious. In practice some company managements (both of large and of smaller firms) seem on occasion to prefer lower risks for themselves rather than higher returns for shareholders.

Adjusting capital structure

How a company invests funds determines its business risk; how it finances them determines its financial risk. A company can adjust its financial risk (gearing) by changing the proportions of debt and equity in its capital structure:

1. *Equity* (a) By retaining profits or paying out dividends;
       (b) by issuing new shares or buying back shares in issue.
2. *Debt* By borrowing money or repaying existing debt.
3. *Both* By converting debt into equity.

These possibilities are set out in Figure 10.6.

In addition to the above, which all involve real cash flows (except the conversion of debt into equity), a company can change its balance sheet capital structure by revaluing assets up or down. Thus revaluing land and buildings upwards has the effect of reducing gearing on the balance sheet; writing off goodwill against reserves has the effect of increasing gearing (by reducing equity). Indeed a few companies have written off so much goodwill that their total shareholders' funds has become negative on the balance sheet, implying gearing of more than 100 per cent. (This is always possible

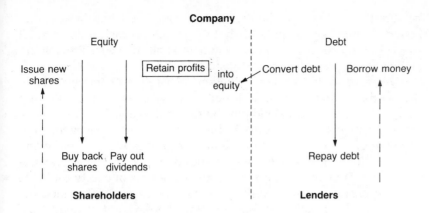

Figure 10.6   Events that change capital structure

using the formula: debt/equity – but it does look odd using the formula: debt/(debt + equity).)

The corporate life cycle

The approach in this sub-section is adapted (with permission) from K. R. Ward, *Corporate Financial Strategy* (Butterworth-Heinemann, 1993).

Start-up

Most business start-ups involve high risk. There may be difficult technical problems to overcome. Even if the product 'works', can the firm make it for a low enough cost? And – crucially important – will enough customers want to buy it? Such high *business* risks suggest that it would be a mistake to pile much (if any) financial risk on top. Indeed most start-ups should probably be financed entirely with equity capital, and have no interest-bearing debt at all.

In any event, debt might be expensive, because it would carry a high risk premium. Most businesses make no taxable profit in the first year or two, implying no tax shield for debt interest, which would therefore have to be paid gross of tax. And since a start-up business probably has mostly intangible assets, with little resale value if anything goes wrong, the costs of 'financial distress' could be very high. Moreover the high risk of complete failure means that a start-up business is quite likely to generate no cash inflows at all from operations. In which case any debt at all, however little, could almost at once lead to severe financial distress.

Investors should not mind whether their returns come by way of dividends or capital gains. So it normally makes sense for a start-up business to pay no dividends in the first few years. It will probably have negative cash flows to begin with. Given a policy of zero borrowing, it would need to raise more equity capital to replace any cash dividends it did pay – which sounds silly. And since transaction costs are mostly fixed, raising small amounts of equity capital is very expensive. In any event, new companies may often lack the post-tax profits legally needed to permit the payment of dividends. And the cash cost of dividends includes advance corporation tax (ACT). If there is not enough mainstream corporation tax payable later to set the ACT off against, that makes paying dividends even more expensive.

Growth

If a start-up business gets over the first hurdle, the risk will decline. But a 'successful' new business will often be growing fast, and thirsty for cash. It will probably still be best to keep debt low, and to proceed to raise additional equity capital in one of three ways: retention of substantially all the profits; a rights issue to existing shareholders; or a launch of the business to the public. The third method will also enable the founding venture capitalists to realize their investment.

Heavy discretionary investment in technical research and in promotion of the new product may restrict book profits at this stage. In any event, capital allowances on heavy investment in fixed assets (which may be needed to expand production) may keep *taxable* profits very low or negative. Assuming that substantial business risks still remain, and with the possible continuing lack of a tax shield on debt interest, borrowing at this stage may still be expensive. But the costs of financial distress should be declining from their previous very high levels, as the business starts to acquire tangible fixed assets with some definite resale value.

With a continuing need to finance rapid growth, the most obvious source of funds is internally generated cash. This implies that dividends should still be zero. But if the company is thinking of going public in the near future, it may wish to start paying a nominal dividend to build up a track record.

Maturity

Once the company reaches maturity, with the rapid growth phase over, profits should start becoming fairly steady. Dividends can now increase and represent a significant proportion of profits. Although existing fixed assets may need to be replaced, in the absence of rapid inflation most of the consequent financial requirement should be able to be met out of provisions for depreciation. (If there were no real growth, in principle the firm should be able to pay out all real profits in dividends.)

With the company now well established, business risk should be fairly low, which should enable it to substitute debt for equity. This may even mean borrowing in effect to increase dividend payments – in order to adjust the capital structure more quickly.

The potential conflict between managers and shareholders will be apparent. High dividends and fairly high debt ratios at this stage may help to maximize shareholders' wealth. But managers may be tempted to retain too much profit and use some of the funds to diversify in order to reduce their own personal risk. Unless there are genuine competitive advantages in doing so, shareholders would probably prefer to do their own diversifying by means of holding a portfolio of securities. It is not easy, however, for shareholders to put pressure on managers to increase the level of dividend payout (or, indeed, the proportionate level of debt).

Decline

In the declining phase, managers should prolong the company's life as long as it can generate positive cash flows that exceed a reasonable rate of return on the net realizable value of the assets. Whether or not to replace fixed assets becomes a genuine question, whereas earlier the main questions may have been when to replace them, and with what modifications (if any).

Internal cash flows will probably exceed reported profits, since depreciation expense may well exceed new investment in replacement fixed assets. Thus dividends paid may even exceed reported profits, and run down the cumulative balance retained in earlier years. (An offsetting influence may be the unwinding of deferred tax provisions from earlier years, which may have reduced reported profits in earlier years but only now result in cash outflows.)

Levels of debt, too, should be high at this stage, since lenders may be able to assess with considerable accuracy the realizable value of any assets against which they are lending.

As suggested above, the main strategic difficulty in the closing stages may be not with shareholders or lenders, but with the managers themselves – who are often (not surprisingly) reluctant to announce simply, 'Our work is done', and then retire gracefully!

11

Mergers and reconstructions

Reasons for mergers

Reasons for buying

'Mergers' and 'acquisitions' both combine two or more separate businesses into one enterprise, with a single top management and common ownership. The term 'merger' often covers both. Strictly, in a **merger** two companies M and N pool all their assets and liabilities; and shareholders exchange their shares in M or N for shares in a new **holding company** MN. In an **acquisition**, A buys all (or most) of the equity shares, of the (net) assets, in B. The purchase price may comprise cash, which buys out the previous ownership interests in B, or shares in A.

The main arguments for mergers are economies of scale, and transferring control of resources to better managers. The main arguments against are the dangers of monopoly, or less competition leading to waste. It is not clear a priori whether higher concentration in an industry will increase or reduce competition: one needs to look at relevant markets, including imports, not merely at domestic production; and one must also consider the impact of *potential* competition.

Most mergers are **horizontal**, combining firms in the same business: for example, a daily newspaper merging with a Sunday. They are most likely to lead to economies of scale, but they may also tend towards monopoly. Economies of scale vary between industries. They need not apply only to production: there may be savings in marketing, research, and even finance. Size can also bring important drawbacks: remoteness of management control; extra layers of overhead cost; and rigid bureaucracy.

Vertical mergers combine firms at different stages of production in the same 'industry'. They may aim to control quality, or to ensure sources of supply or retail outlets. Thus a producer of soft drinks might combine 'upstream' with fruit growers or a company making containers, or 'downstream' with a firm operating ice cream vans.

Conglomerate mergers combine firms in different industries, perhaps with no obvious connection: for example, a cigarette maker and an insurance company, or a drinks manufacturer and a chain of opticians. Such mergers are fairly rare. Economic benefits might stem from tax savings, management skills in the centre, or financial efficiencies. It can be hard to interpret **group accounts (consolidated accounts)** which add together numbers from different industries. Hence SSAP 25 requires groups to report separately their sales, profits and assets in the various different industry segments in which they operate.

The acquiring company may want expansion *more quickly* than by internal growth. In some industries size may be essential to compete globally. There may be a desire to avoid outside control: it is much harder for governments to interfere with intragroup transactions than with 'visible' market deals between autonomous companies. (This may be an important reason for international combinations.) Table 11.1 sets out a number of possible reasons for one business to acquire another, which may overlap.

Reasons for selling

Many commercial assets are for sale if 'the price is right', even if the owners were not planning to sell. People who have founded a business, or inherited it, may want either to retire or to spread their investment risk. They can defer any capital gains tax bill by receiving shares rather than cash; and if they accept shares in a listed company, they can dispose of them whenever they choose.

Another reason for selling a business may be management problems, either succession or lack of ability to manage a larger business following a period of growth. The death or retirement of one or two key people can often reveal a need for new management. Sometimes selling an ailing business may simply be 'a civilized alternative to **bankruptcy**'. Sale as a going concern will normally

Table 11.1 Reasons for acquisition

Production
1. Expanding capacity.
2. Economies of scale.
3. Acquiring technology.
4. Vertical integration, for quality control or supply reasons.

Marketing
5. Expanding market share.
6. Extending product range.
7. Gaining entry to new markets.
8. Eliminating competition.
9. Vertical integration, for distribution reasons.

Miscellaneous
10. Target company's shares or assets 'under-priced'.
11. Acquirer's shares 'over-valued'.
12. Applying superior management skills to the acquiree's business.
13. Acquiring management skills to apply to the acquirer's business.
14. Preventing a competitor from acquiring the target company.
15. Making the acquiring company itself less attractive to a predator.
16. Tax benefits (such as ACT).
17. Avoiding government interference.
18. Diversifying business risk.
19. Empire building.

produce a better price than winding a firm up; and it will avoid many human and legal problems.

Selling a division of a group of companies may make strategic sense if it no longer fits with the core business, or if the group needs extra finance for the rest of its business. It may also make the vendor company less attractive to a predator. Table 11.2 lists reasons for selling a company.

Management versus shareholders

Managers are likely to have all their eggs in the one basket, so they may be keen to merge to reduce their company's *total* risk. In theory this makes no sense for a company's *owners* if they hold a portfolio of shares and can thus diversify away most of any company's 'unique risk' (see Chapter 9). (But owners of family companies may not be in this position.)

Getting into new areas of business may be exciting for managers, but it may also involve big risks. On average, acquiring groups have

Table 11.2   Reasons for selling (part of) a business

Ownership
1.   Owner wants to diversify risk.
2.   Owner wants to reduce tax problems on death.

Management
3.   Manager(s) about to retire, with no obvious successor.
4.   Poor business prospects under control of present management, possibly following expansion or a change of direction.

Part of a group
5.   Needs extra source of finance.
6.   No longer fits with core business or strategy of vendor group.
7.   Make *vendor* less attractive to a predator.

Miscellaneous
8.   Needs economies of scale (might justify *acquisition* rather than sale!).
9.   Vendor's shares or assets 'over-valued'.

---

to pay a 25 per cent premium on the vendor's (pre-bid) share price. This may absorb nearly all the economic gains from the merger, leaving little if any reward for shareholders in the acquiring group.

Managers may welcome size for its own sake if their pay partly depends on it, whereas shareholders want a good rate of return on equity. That is why shareholders would often prefer a higher dividend payout ratio than the top managers. Merging may also improve a group's credit rating, which may make life more comfortable for managers.

Poor managers, who fail to maximize shareholder wealth, ought in the end to be vulnerable to a takeover bid for control of their company. That could yield large profits for those who organize such a bid. They could either run the business better themselves, or else split it up and sell parts of it off. Private companies, however, may not be easy to take over; hence they are high-risk investments, certainly for **minority** shareholders. In practice, though, even for listed companies, the short-term pressures on incompetent or unlucky managers may be less than theory suggests.

Joint ventures and minority interests

So far we have been discussing mergers and acquisitions on the basis that they involve 100 per cent of a company's equity shares.

But share deals between 'partners' may involve less than 100 per cent of the equity, especially in international transactions.

For example, if a company wishes to expand into a foreign country, it may make sense to proceed by way of joint venture or minority interest. In a joint venture, each of two partners owns 50 per cent of the equity. Under the so-called equity basis, the accounts normally show the investment at cost plus any share of retained profits, while the profit and loss account reports the share of profits or losses (not just dividends received, if any).

Where only a minority interest in the equity is held, the equity basis of accounting is still normally used if the share of equity held is at least 20 per cent. The investment is then said to be in an **associated company** (or 'related company').

Why would a company choose to own only a minority interest, rather than 100 per cent of the equity? Such an arrangement does, of course, reduce the amount it needs to invest in an enterprise of any given size. More important, however, is probably to benefit from the foreign partner's local knowhow and connections.

There may be dangers. Not all cultures may see such relationships in the same light. British Aerospace sold its 80 per cent interest in Rover to the German company BMW, which upset the Japanese company Honda who owned 20 per cent of Rover's equity. British Aerospace seemed to regard its 80/20 'partnership' with Honda as mainly financial, to be ditched if and when a 'better deal' came along; whereas Honda believed their 20 per cent interest in Rover was a long-term arrangement.

In one sense, a minority interest, or investment in a joint venture, may resemble an 'option' (see Chapter 6). It may give an investing company a springboard for developing 100 per cent interests in the country (or industry) concerned, when it has learned enough (and also when it has begun to establish a local reputation of its own). On the other hand the local partner may be gaining access to foreign technology. On this view, joint ventures and minority interests may often turn out *not* to be long-term arrangements.

Merger statistics

Figure 11.1 portrays (in constant March 1994 pounds) the annual total costs of UK acquisitions for each of the twenty-five years between 1969 and 1993. The average annual cost was £10 billion. In 1972 acquisitions cost £17 billion, nearly twice the average; but

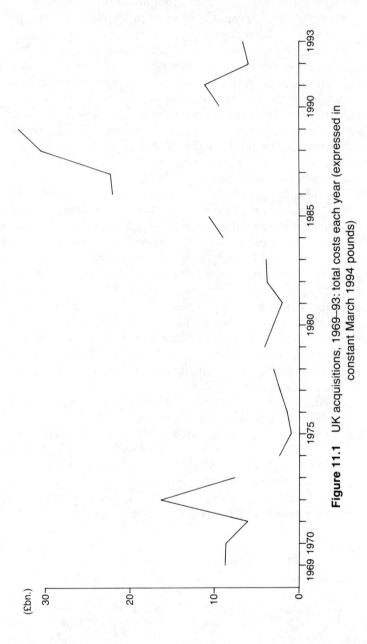

Figure 11.1   UK acquisitions, 1969–93: total costs each year (expressed in constant March 1994 pounds)

Table 11.3 Summary of UK acquisitions 1969–93, and means of payment

	Average annual totals			Split of purchase price (%)		
	Number of years	Number of acquisitions	Cost in 1994 £bn.	Cash	Shares	Loans, etc.
1969–73	5	990	9.7	28	51	21
1974–78	5	440	2.2	63	33	4
1979–83	5	470	3.5	54	39	7
1984–85	2	520	9.7	46	44	10
1986–89	4	1,300	27.4	57	35	8
1990–93	4	560	8.4	73	25	2
1969–93	25	720	9.6	53	37	10

during the ten years 1974–83 the total cost averaged only £3 billion a year. Between 1986 and 1989 the total averaged £27 billion a year. The total cost of acquisitions during the five years 1985–9 exceeded the total cost in the remaining twenty years of the period; and the average size of acquisitions in these five years (£21 million) was more than twice as much as in the other twenty years.

Table 11.3 summarizes the annual averages, and analyzes the means of payment. In the first four years of the period, 54 per cent of the total costs were paid in equity shares, 24 per cent in cash and 22 per cent in loans, etc. The pattern was similar in the three years 1985–7, with 58 per cent paid in equity shares, 32 per cent in cash and only 10 per cent in loans, etc. But in the other eighteen years, only 25 per cent of the costs were paid in equity shares, no less than 69 per cent in cash, and only 6 per cent in loan stock and preference shares.

The process of merging

Valuation

An acquiring company may regard an acquisition as a capital investment 'project'. The amount of the investment is the purchase price, plus any extra amount which the acquirer plans to invest in the business, less the disposal proceeds of any surplus assets. The assets being acquired may be equity shares in the holding company of a group, the assets of the group, or the assets of part of a group. Specified liabilities may also be taken over. Estimates of the acquisition project's future cash flows should allow for **synergy**, or other expected changes, as well as for any further investment. The acquirer may also wish to allow for some terminal value at the horizon date. To find the maximum purchase price payable, the acquirer can discount the estimated future cash flows to present value. The discount rate should represent the rate of return suitable for the riskiness of the business being acquired (which may not be the same as the acquirer's).

As a check on valuations reached in this way, it may be useful to employ other valuation methods too, such as price/earnings ratios or even book values of assets. For listed companies it has been common for the purchase price to average some 25 per cent more than the pre-bid market price per share. This may often leave a demanding task for the acquirer's management to earn a profit on top of that premium.

Bargaining

In a 'friendly' deal, an acquirer (A) will try to find out why the seller (S) wants to sell. Is S aware of adverse future factors which A does not know about? Or are there personal reasons for selling? And S will try to discover A's motives. Does A value some aspect of the business more highly than S? If so, why? And how much is it worth to A?

Both A and S should take care throughout to keep an eye on possible alternatives. A will be comparing S with other possible purchases, or with internal growth. S will be looking around for other possible buyers, or on continuing ownership. If there seems to be no feasible alternative, it will be hard to drive much of a bargain.

Both buyer and seller may have in mind a range of suitable prices. If they overlap, a deal should be possible. Of course the range may alter during the bargaining. In the excitement of an auction, a 'successful' buyer can end up paying far more than he planned; or this may be the price of keeping a deal 'friendly'. The ability to walk away from a deal that is costing too much may not win much glory, but perhaps it serves the interests of shareholders better than overexpensive 'triumphs'.

Basing the purchase price partly on future profits defers some of the cost and reduces the risk, by protecting the buyer if promised future profits fail to occur. It may also act as an incentive for former owner-managers to continue working well. On the other hand, this kind of arrangement can turn out very messy if the acquired business is reorganized or combined with some of the buyer's existing business units.

In hostile takeover bids, the interests of the victim's (V) top management may not coincide with those of V's shareholders. The management may prefer continuing independence at almost any price. The City Code which governs takeover practice requires V's directors to provide full details of any offer to enable V's shareholders to make an informed decision.

Financing

Combining two formerly separate companies is likely to increase the total equity 'cushion', and thus to reduce the risk for existing creditors. Indeed, by reducing an enterprise's *total* risk (though not perhaps its *market* risk – see Chapter 9), merging may encourage management to increase financial gearing.

The method of payment will affect financial structure. For instance, a company with a 35 per cent debt ratio which acquires another company half its size could end up with a debt ratio varying from 23 per cent to 57 per cent, depending whether none or all of the purchase price were borrowed. (The price might *consist* of loan stock in the acquiring group; or the acquiring group might borrow itself in order to finance a purchase for cash.)

A well-known advantage of paying in equity shares is to delay any capital gains tax liability for the vendors, and to enable any such liability to be spread out over time. There is some dispute whether the accounting treatment of any **goodwill** arising on an acquisition matters or not. Goodwill is defined as the excess of the purchase price over the fair value of the separable net assets acquired. Under SSAP 22 (now being revised) UK companies may **write off** goodwill immediately against reserves (and nearly all do so). UK companies are permitted to follow the usual international requirement, of capitalizing goodwill and then amortizing it against profit over a limited period, but this is not very popular with company directors.

Human consequences

Over time most companies develop a style of their own; and it can be difficult to combine two firms with different cultures. (The history of the European Common Market illustrates the same point on a national scale!) Making a merger work takes a great deal of management time and effort. Depending on the nature of the merger (is it horizontal, vertical, or conglomerate?), the new group's top management may wish to look in some detail at every significant aspect of the business being acquired: each major product line, every plant, the main markets, all senior personnel.

Human problems often arise among workers as a result of a merger. 'Economies of scale' may be an abstract way of saying that one person can do two people's jobs. So the other person may have to go. Other employees may be demoted, or have to move to a new office or factory, perhaps far away from their present home and friends. Such 'redeployment' may often make good economic sense, but to implement it requires great skill, understanding and tact on management's part. Experience suggests that to avoid unnecessary uncertainty it is usually important to tell the workers in a newly acquired business as much as possible as soon as possible about future plans.

Restructuring

Privatization

During the decade 1984 to 1993 the British government **privatized** many of the state-owned industries, including electricity, gas, telecommunications and water. This amounted to a major change for the whole economy. Of the 100 largest UK companies in 1994, about one-quarter had been in the state sector in 1979.

The main reason was to increase competition, and to make a number of important industries more responsive to their customers. According to the government, it would be a waste 'merely to replace state monopolies by private ones'. Other motives were: to reduce political interference with management; to end the need for the state to finance capital investment; to relieve taxpayers of the burden of bearing losses; to raise money for the government; and to increase the number of personal shareholders. Some of these objectives clashed. Selling a monopoly would yield higher proceeds than making an industry more competitive first. The government wanted large numbers of people to apply for shares and underpriced several offers for sale, thus raising less money than possible.

The process has involved splitting industries, reforming capital structures, strengthening boards of directors, setting up new systems of regulation (such as OFTEL, OFWAT, and so on), and marketing the shares. By 1994 the government was planning to sell off several of the following industries still under state control: Atomic Energy, Coal, London Regional Transport, Nuclear Electric, the Post Office, the Railways, and the Waterways.

Since 1984 the proceeds from selling off state enterprises have totalled about $_{94}$£70 billion (i.e. in 1994 purchasing power) – nearly half the total amount spent on acquiring UK companies. The scale of the transfer from the public sector has been enormous: in the larger enterprises, the government sold its 100 per cent holding in two or three tranches; and applicants for the shares paid for each tranche by instalments.

Demerging

Recent changes in company law and tax law, as well as in corporate management fashions, have led to a number of 'demergers'. There are three main versions: trade sales, spin-offs, and management buy-outs.

Trade sales

From time to time a group may want to sell one of its divisions. This may be because someone has offered a high price (for example, Grand Met selling its hotels); or to avoid the need to finance heavy future investment (for example, British Aerospace selling Rover); or to dispose of a loss-making business with poor prospects under existing management. In such cases, selling to another company in the same industry may make a lot of sense.

A parent may have to make large write-offs in order to leave a poorly performing business viable; but selling it relieves the parent of future losses without all the costs of winding it up. For instance when selling Jaguar and British Airways to the public, the government wrote down their fixed assets in a big way. This made it easier for them to report accounting profits afterwards, though it did not affect the cash flows (see Chapter 3).

In the state sector, a number of small privatizations were sales to trade buyers, rather than public offers for sale: for example, British Rail Hotels and International Aeradio. The government may use the same approach for British Coal, which is now only a small business.

Spin-offs

With a **spin-off**, the holding company distributes shares in a **subsidiary** pro rata to its own shareholders. This may be a substantial business in its own right, and thereafter have a separate stock market listing. Recent examples include: Courtaulds Textiles (Courtaulds), Vodafone (Racal Electronics), and Zeneca (Imperial Chemical Industries).

Demergers may make sense where two businesses are not closely related, and enjoy few if any economies of scale; though some conglomerate managers must believe that they can add value somehow, perhaps by systems of financial control, or skill at buying and selling companies. The arrangement which first joined the two businesses together may even have been a mistake: for example (perhaps), BAT Industries (tobacco and insurance). Rothmans International has recently spun-off its non-tobacco interests, and there are rumours (since denied) that Philip Morris plans to do the same.

There are examples of demerger in the state sector too. At one time the Post Office included what is now British Telecom. Both National Power and Powergen, as well as Nuclear Electric, came from the former Central Electricity Generating Board. And the regional water companies, which used to be a single centrally controlled industry, are now independent businesses.

Management buy-outs

A holding company wishing to sell a business may seek a trade buyer, or for large companies it may consider a spin-off. But sometimes the best offer may come from its existing managers. They may recognize its potential better than anyone else. In a **management buy-out (MBO)** the management team arranges to buy an equity stake in the business. Venture capitalists back them by putting up the rest of the purchase price. This is partly equity, and often mostly loan capital.

Because the new company is often highly geared, Americans call such deals leveraged buy-outs (LBOs). This makes them risky, but needing most of the cash flow to service the debt pressures the management team to perform. If they do so, they can make large capital gains from their equity stake. This may not be a large proportion of the company's total capital, but it will nearly always represent a substantial part of their personal wealth.

There is an obvious moral hazard here for managers of a subsidiary company. They may be tempted to do less than their best while part of a larger group, in order to benefit themselves by buying an equity stake cheap. The danger may be even stronger if a

Table 11.4 UK MBOs (and MBIs) > £10 million 1986–93 (Source: KPMG, April 1994, with RPI adjustments)

Year	Number	Total value
1986	27	1.4
1987	33	3.8
1988	55	6.0
1989	72	7.3
1990	60	2.3
1991	44	2.0
1992	54	2.4
1993	51	2.0

Note: March 1994 £billion.

management team plans to buy out the whole group, rather than just a part of it.

Recent examples of private sector management buy-outs are: Del Monte Foods, Midlands Newspapers, and Gardner Merchant. An early example from the state sector was the National Freight Corporation.

In a variant, a management *buy-in*, a management team from *outside* an enterprise offers to buy it. Venture capitalists back the team, as in MBOs. In such cases there is no moral hazard, but outsiders will not know the business as well as inside managers. Table 11.4 summarizes MBOs since 1986. It contains three £1 billion deals (in 1994 pounds): MFI/Hygena (1987) £1.0 billion; Redpack (1988) £1.1 billion; and Gateway (1989, MBI) £2.9 billion.

Reducing equity capital

A company with a deficit on profit and loss account may legally be unable to pay dividends out of current profits. For that reason, or before raising new capital, it may be necessary to reduce its equity capital to eliminate such deficits.

Reducing capital requires the agreement of the court, mainly to safeguard the interests of creditors. Where the share capital is lost, or not backed by assets, the creditors need not suffer from formal acknowledgement of the facts.

A recent private sector example is British Aerospace reducing its share capital by £750 million to recognize a special loss of that amount in 1992. It cancelled £599 million of share premium, and wrote £151 million off its paid-up share capital by reducing the nominal amount of 377 million ordinary shares from 50p to 10p each.

Several nationalized industries have written off huge losses: for example, British Airways, British Coal, British Rail and British Steel. However, since the government was the major loan creditor as well as the 100 per cent equity owner, no major conflict of interest arose. (In adjusting nationalized industry accounts for inflation by the **CPP** method, I treated government debt as equity, thus avoiding the need to credit 'gains' on **monetary liabilities**.)

Liquidation

Liquidation (or winding-up) is a legal process, triggered by **insolvency** (failure to pay debts due). It involves:

1. The appointment of a liquidator.
2. Disposing of all the assets for cash.
3. Sharing out the cash proceeds among creditors and (perhaps) shareholders.

Members of a company can choose to wind it up (voluntary liquidation). The effect of a compulsory liquidation is to remove resources from the control of managements which have made losses or mismanaged their company's finances. (Lack of profit, of course, is not the same thing as lack of cash.) Not all firms which lose money go into liquidation: the higher the proportion of equity in the capital structure, the lower the chance of that.

Figure 11.2 shows that 'compulsory' liquidations in the UK have risen sharply, from about 4,000 a year in the early 1970s to an

---

Table 11.5 Priority of distribution on a liquidation

1. Costs of liquidation
2. Creditors secured by a fixed charge on property
3. 'Preferential' creditors:
    (a) one year's taxes due to government
    (b) wages of employees
4. Creditors secured by a floating charge
5. Unsecured creditors
6. Preference shareholders
7. Ordinary shareholders

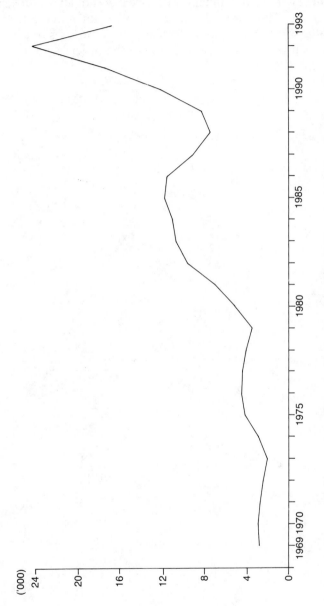

Figure 11.2 Company liquidations, both compulsory and creditors' voluntary, in England and Wales, 1969–93

average of around 12,000 a year in the late 1980s. A peak of 24,000 was reached in 1992.

When a firm goes into liquidation its assets do not all disappear in a puff of smoke! They are sold for cash, often for much less than their balance sheet book amounts (though sometimes for much more). The cash proceeds are distributed in the order listed in Table 11.5.

Appendix A
Acronyms

AC	Annualized cost
ACT	Advance corporation tax
BV	Book value
CAPM	Capital asset pricing model
CCA	Current cost accounting
CGT	Capital gains tax
CH	Compounding to horizon
COGS	Cost of goods sold
CPP	Constant purchasing power
CT	Corporation tax
DCF	Discounted cash flow
DPR	Dividend payout ratio
DY	Dividend yield
EPS	Earnings per share
ERM	Exchange rate mechanism
EVA	Economic value added
EY	Earnings yield
FIFO	First in, first out
FRS	Financial reporting standard
HC	Historical cost
HP	Hire purchase

| IPO | Initial public offering |
| IRR | Internal rate of return |

| LIFO | Last in, first out |
| Ltd | Limited (company) |

MBI	Management buy-in
MBO	Management buy-out
MI	Minority interests
MPT	Modern portfolio theory

NBV	Net book value
NPV	Net present value
NRV	Net realizable value
NTV	Net terminal value

PBIT	Profit before interest and tax
P/E	Price/earnings (multiple or ratio)
PI	Profitability index
P&L	Profit and loss
PLC	Public limited company
PPP	Purchasing power parity
PV	Present value

R_f	Risk-free (rate of return)
RI	Residual income
R_m	Return on the market
ROCE	Return on capital employed
ROFE	Return on funds employed
ROI	Return on investment
RONA	Return on net assets
RPI	Retail prices index

| SEAQ | Stock Exchange Automated Quotations |
| SSAP | Statement of Standard Accounting Practice |

| USM | Unlisted securities market |

| VAT | Value added tax |

WACC	Weighted average cost of capital
wda	writing-down allowance
WIP	Work in progress

Appendix B
Present value tables

Table A Present value of £1

Years Hence	1%	2%	4%	6%	8%	10%	12%	14%	15%	16%	18%	20%	22%	24%	25%	26%	28%	30%	35%	40%	45%	50%
1	0.990	0.980	0.962	0.943	0.926	0.909	0.893	0.877	0.870	0.862	0.847	0.833	0.820	0.806	0.800	0.794	0.781	0.769	0.741	0.714	0.690	0.667
2	0.980	0.961	0.925	0.890	0.857	0.826	0.797	0.769	0.756	0.743	0.718	0.694	0.672	0.650	0.640	0.630	0.610	0.592	0.549	0.510	0.476	0.444
3	0.971	0.942	0.889	0.840	0.794	0.751	0.712	0.675	0.658	0.641	0.609	0.579	0.551	0.524	0.512	0.500	0.477	0.455	0.406	0.364	0.328	0.296
4	0.961	0.924	0.855	0.792	0.735	0.683	0.636	0.592	0.572	0.552	0.516	0.482	0.451	0.423	0.410	0.397	0.373	0.350	0.301	0.260	0.226	0.198
5	0.951	0.906	0.822	0.747	0.681	0.621	0.567	0.519	0.497	0.476	0.437	0.402	0.370	0.341	0.328	0.315	0.291	0.269	0.223	0.186	0.156	0.132
6	0.942	0.888	0.790	0.705	0.630	0.564	0.507	0.456	0.432	0.410	0.370	0.335	0.303	0.275	0.262	0.250	0.227	0.207	0.165	0.133	0.108	0.088
7	0.933	0.871	0.760	0.665	0.583	0.513	0.452	0.400	0.376	0.354	0.314	0.279	0.249	0.222	0.210	0.198	0.178	0.159	0.122	0.095	0.074	0.059
8	0.923	0.853	0.731	0.627	0.540	0.467	0.404	0.351	0.327	0.305	0.266	0.233	0.204	0.179	0.168	0.157	0.139	0.123	0.091	0.068	0.051	0.039
9	0.914	0.837	0.703	0.592	0.500	0.424	0.361	0.308	0.284	0.263	0.225	0.194	0.167	0.144	0.134	0.125	0.108	0.094	0.067	0.048	0.035	0.026
10	0.905	0.820	0.676	0.558	0.463	0.386	0.322	0.270	0.247	0.227	0.191	0.162	0.137	0.116	0.107	0.099	0.085	0.073	0.050	0.035	0.024	0.017
11	0.896	0.804	0.650	0.527	0.429	0.350	0.287	0.237	0.215	0.195	0.162	0.135	0.112	0.094	0.086	0.079	0.066	0.056	0.037	0.025	0.017	0.012
12	0.887	0.788	0.625	0.497	0.397	0.319	0.257	0.208	0.187	0.168	0.137	0.112	0.092	0.076	0.069	0.062	0.052	0.043	0.027	0.018	0.012	0.008
13	0.879	0.773	0.601	0.469	0.368	0.290	0.229	0.182	0.163	0.145	0.116	0.093	0.075	0.061	0.055	0.050	0.040	0.033	0.020	0.013	0.008	0.005
14	0.870	0.758	0.577	0.442	0.340	0.263	0.205	0.160	0.141	0.125	0.099	0.078	0.062	0.049	0.044	0.039	0.032	0.025	0.015	0.009	0.006	0.003
15	0.861	0.743	0.555	0.417	0.315	0.239	0.183	0.140	0.123	0.108	0.084	0.065	0.051	0.040	0.035	0.031	0.025	0.020	0.011	0.006	0.004	0.002

16	0.853	0.728	0.534	0.394	0.292	0.218	0.163	0.123	0.107	0.093	0.071	0.054	0.042	0.032	0.028	0.025	0.019	0.015	0.008	0.005	0.003	0.002
17	0.844	0.714	0.513	0.371	0.270	0.198	0.146	0.108	0.093	0.080	0.060	0.045	0.034	0.026	0.023	0.020	0.015	0.012	0.006	0.003	0.002	0.001
18	0.836	0.700	0.494	0.350	0.250	0.180	0.130	0.095	0.081	0.069	0.051	0.038	0.028	0.021	0.018	0.016	0.012	0.009	0.005	0.002	0.001	0.001
19	0.828	0.686	0.475	0.331	0.232	0.164	0.116	0.083	0.070	0.060	0.043	0.031	0.023	0.017	0.014	0.012	0.009	0.007	0.003	0.002	0.001	
20	0.820	0.673	0.456	0.312	0.215	0.149	0.104	0.073	0.061	0.051	0.037	0.026	0.019	0.014	0.012	0.010	0.007	0.005	0.002	0.001	0.001	
21	0.811	0.660	0.439	0.294	0.199	0.135	0.093	0.064	0.053	0.044	0.031	0.022	0.015	0.011	0.009	0.008	0.006	0.004	0.002	0.001		
22	0.803	0.647	0.422	0.278	0.184	0.123	0.083	0.056	0.046	0.038	0.026	0.018	0.013	0.009	0.007	0.006	0.004	0.003	0.001	0.001		
23	0.795	0.634	0.406	0.262	0.170	0.112	0.074	0.049	0.040	0.033	0.022	0.015	0.010	0.007	0.006	0.005	0.003	0.002	0.001			
24	0.788	0.622	0.390	0.247	0.158	0.102	0.066	0.043	0.035	0.028	0.019	0.013	0.008	0.006	0.005	0.004	0.003	0.002	0.001			
25	0.780	0.610	0.375	0.233	0.146	0.092	0.059	0.038	0.030	0.024	0.016	0.010	0.007	0.005	0.004	0.003	0.002	0.001	0.001			
26	0.772	0.598	0.361	0.220	0.135	0.084	0.053	0.033	0.026	0.021	0.014	0.009	0.006	0.004	0.003	0.002	0.002	0.001	0.001			
27	0.764	0.586	0.347	0.207	0.125	0.076	0.047	0.029	0.023	0.018	0.011	0.007	0.005	0.003	0.002	0.001	0.001	0.001				
28	0.757	0.574	0.333	0.196	0.116	0.069	0.042	0.026	0.020	0.016	0.010	0.006	0.004	0.002	0.002	0.002	0.001	0.001				
29	0.749	0.563	0.321	0.185	0.107	0.063	0.037	0.022	0.017	0.014	0.008	0.005	0.003	0.002	0.002	0.001	0.001	0.001				
30	0.742	0.552	0.308	0.174	0.099	0.057	0.033	0.020	0.015	0.012	0.007	0.004	0.003	0.002	0.001	0.001						
40	0.672	0.453	0.208	0.097	0.046	0.022	0.011	0.005	0.004	0.003	0.001											
50	0.608	0.372	0.141	0.054	0.021	0.009	0.003	0.001	0.001	0.001												

Table B Present value of £1 received annually for N years

Years Hence	1%	2%	4%	6%	8%	10%	12%	14%	15%	16%	18%	20%	22%	24%	25%	26%	28%	30%	35%	40%	45%	50%
1	0.990	0.980	0.962	0.943	0.926	0.909	0.893	0.877	0.870	0.862	0.847	0.833	0.820	0.806	0.800	0.794	0.781	0.769	0.741	0.714	0.690	0.667
2	1.970	1.942	1.886	1.833	1.783	1.736	1.690	1.647	1.626	1.605	1.566	1.528	1.492	1.457	1.440	1.424	1.392	1.361	1.289	1.224	1.165	1.111
3	2.941	2.884	2.773	2.673	2.577	2.487	2.402	2.322	2.283	2.246	2.174	2.106	2.042	1.981	1.952	1.923	1.868	1.816	1.696	1.589	1.493	1.407
4	3.902	3.808	3.630	3.465	3.312	3.170	3.037	2.914	2.855	2.798	2.690	2.589	2.494	2.404	2.362	2.320	2.241	2.166	1.997	1.849	1.720	1.605
5	4.853	4.713	4.452	4.212	3.993	3.791	3.605	3.433	3.352	3.274	3.127	2.991	2.864	2.745	2.689	2.635	2.532	2.436	2.220	2.035	1.876	1.737
6	5.795	5.601	5.242	4.917	4.623	4.355	4.111	3.889	3.784	3.685	3.498	3.326	3.167	3.020	2.951	2.885	2.759	2.643	2.385	2.168	1.983	1.824
7	6.728	6.472	6.002	5.582	5.206	4.868	4.564	4.288	4.160	4.039	3.812	3.605	3.416	3.242	3.161	3.083	2.937	2.802	2.508	2.263	2.057	1.883
8	7.652	7.325	6.733	6.210	5.747	5.335	4.968	4.639	4.487	4.344	4.078	3.837	3.619	3.421	3.329	3.241	3.076	2.925	2.598	2.331	2.108	1.922
9	8.566	8.162	7.435	6.802	6.247	5.759	5.328	4.946	4.772	4.607	4.303	4.031	3.786	3.566	3.463	3.366	3.184	3.019	2.665	2.379	2.144	1.948
10	9.471	8.983	8.111	7.360	6.710	6.145	5.650	5.216	5.019	4.833	4.494	4.192	3.923	3.682	3.571	3.465	3.269	3.092	2.715	2.414	2.168	1.965
11	10.368	9.787	8.760	7.887	7.139	6.495	5.937	5.453	5.234	5.029	4.656	4.327	4.035	3.776	3.656	3.544	3.335	3.147	2.757	2.438	2.185	1.977
12	11.255	10.573	9.385	8.384	7.536	6.814	6.194	5.660	5.421	5.197	4.793	4.439	4.127	3.851	3.725	3.606	3.387	3.190	2.779	2.456	2.196	1.985
13	12.134	11.343	9.986	8.853	7.904	7.103	6.424	5.842	5.583	5.342	4.910	4.533	4.203	3.912	3.780	3.656	3.427	3.223	2.799	2.468	2.204	1.990
14	13.004	12.106	10.563	9.295	8.244	7.367	6.628	6.002	5.724	5.468	5.008	4.611	4.265	3.962	3.824	3.695	3.459	3.249	2.814	2.477	2.210	1.993
15	13.865	12.849	11.118	9.712	8.559	7.606	6.811	6.142	5.847	5.575	5.092	4.675	4.315	4.001	3.859	3.726	3.483	3.268	2.825	2.484	2.214	1.995

16	14.718	13.578	11.652	10.106	8.851	7.824	6.974	6.265	5.954	5.669	5.162	4.730	4.357	4.033	3.887	3.751	3.503	3.283	2.834	2.489	2.216	1.997
17	15.562	14.292	12.166	10.477	9.122	8.022	7.120	6.373	6.047	5.749	5.222	4.775	4.391	4.059	3.910	3.771	3.518	3.295	2.840	2.492	2.218	1.998
18	16.398	14.992	12.659	10.828	9.372	8.201	7.250	6.467	6.128	5.818	5.273	4.812	4.419	4.080	3.928	3.786	3.529	3.304	2.844	2.494	2.219	1.999
19	17.226	15.678	13.134	11.158	9.604	8.365	7.366	6.550	6.198	5.877	5.316	4.844	4.442	4.097	3.942	3.799	3.539	3.311	2.848	2.496	2.220	1.999
20	18.046	16.351	13.590	11.470	9.818	8.514	7.469	6.623	6.259	5.929	5.353	4.870	4.460	4.110	3.954	3.808	3.546	3.316	2.850	2.497	2.221	1.999
21	18.857	17.011	14.029	11.764	10.017	8.649	7.562	6.687	6.312	5.973	5.384	4.891	4.476	4.121	3.963	3.816	3.551	3.320	2.852	2.498	2.221	2.000
22	19.660	17.654	14.451	12.042	10.201	8.772	7.645	6.743	6.359	6.011	5.410	4.909	4.488	4.130	3.970	3.822	3.556	3.323	2.853	2.498	2.222	2.000
23	20.456	18.292	14.857	12.303	10.371	8.883	7.718	6.792	6.399	6.044	5.432	4.925	4.499	4.137	3.976	3.827	3.559	3.325	2.854	2.499	2.222	2.000
24	21.243	18.914	15.247	12.550	10.529	8.985	7.784	6.835	6.434	6.073	5.451	4.937	4.507	4.143	3.981	3.831	3.562	3.327	2.855	2.499	2.222	2.000
25	22.023	19.523	15.622	12.783	10.675	9.077	7.843	6.873	6.464	6.097	5.467	4.948	4.514	4.147	3.985	3.834	3.564	3.329	2.856	2.499	2.222	2.000
26	22.795	20.121	15.983	13.003	10.810	9.161	7.896	6.906	6.491	6.118	5.480	4.956	4.520	4.151	3.988	3.837	3.566	3.330	2.856	2.500	2.222	2.000
27	23.560	20.709	16.330	13.211	10.935	9.237	7.943	6.935	6.514	6.136	5.492	4.964	4.524	4.154	3.990	3.839	3.567	3.331	2.856	2.500	2.222	2.000
28	24.316	21.281	16.663	13.406	11.051	9.307	7.984	6.961	6.534	6.152	5.502	4.970	4.528	4.157	3.992	3.840	3.568	3.331	2.857	2.500	2.222	2.000
29	25.066	21.844	16.984	13.591	11.154	9.370	8.022	6.983	6.551	6.166	5.510	4.975	4.531	4.159	3.994	3.841	3.569	3.332	2.857	2.500	2.222	2.000
30	25.808	22.396	17.292	13.765	11.254	9.427	8.065	7.003	6.566	6.177	5.517	4.979	4.534	4.160	3.995	3.842	3.569	3.332	2.857	2.500	2.222	2.000
40	32.835	27.355	19.793	15.046	11.925	9.779	8.244	7.105	6.642	6.234	5.548	4.997	4.544	4.166	3.999	3.846	3.571	3.333	2.857	2.500	2.222	2.000
50	39.196	31.424	21.482	15.762	12.234	9.915	8.304	7.133	6.661	6.246	5.554	4.999	4.545	4.167	4.000	3.846	3.571	3.333	2.857	2.500	2.222	2.000

Glossary

Accounting standards Rules on disclosure and measurement in accounts, formerly issued by Accounting Standards Committee [SSAPs = Statements of Standard Accounting Practice], and since 1990 by Accounting Standards Board [FRSs = Financial Reporting Standards]. See Figure 1.6 for topics covered.

Accounts Profit and loss account for a period, balance sheet as at the end of that period, and notes to the accounts, together with the auditors' report and a cash flow statement.

Accounts payable (creditors) Amounts due to suppliers for goods or services purchased on credit.

Accounts receivable (debtors) Amounts due from customers for goods or services sold on credit.

Accruals concept The accounting principle of recognizing transactions in the period to which they relate, rather than when cash is paid.

Accrued charge Liability not yet invoiced, often relating to period cost.

Acid test ratio Ratio of liquid assets (cash + debtors) divided by current liabilities. Yardstick of a firm's ability to pay its short-term debts.

Acquisition Purchase by one company of another.

Advance corporation tax (ACT) Part of UK corporation tax liability, payable at same time as dividends, set off later against 'mainstream' corporation tax.

Amortization Depreciation, usually of intangible assets.

Annualized cost (AC) Discounted cash flow technique, alternative to capitalizing revenue, which annualizes the initial investment.

Annuity   Regular annual amount for a number of years. For present values, see Appendix B.

Arbitrage   Buying in one market and selling in another to gain from price differences (which the process will reduce but, due to transaction costs, not eliminate).

Asset   Valuable resource which a business owns or controls.

Asset beta (or **ungeared beta**)   Beta of a firm's total assets, rather than of its ordinary shares.

Asset turnover   Annual sales revenue divided by net assets.

Associated company (or **related company**)   An undertaking in which the company has a participating interest. Company in which another company (i) owns between 20 and 50 per cent of the ordinary shares, and (ii) influences management.

Audit   External examination of financial accounts (and records and systems) by independent professional accountants, to report whether accounts give a true and fair view.

Bad debt   Debt reckoned to be uncollectable.

Balance sheet   Classified statement of financial position of a business, showing assets, liabilities, and shareholders' funds at a particular date.

Bank of England   UK central bank responsible for the integrity of the currency. Official 'authority' overseeing City institutions and markets.

Bank overdraft   Amount owing to bank, repayable 'on demand'. Both the amount borrowed, and the rate of interest, may fluctuate.

Bankruptcy   Legal process occurring when a person is unable to pay due debts. Equivalent for companies is liquidation (i.e. winding-up).

Bear   Speculator expecting prices to fall, who may sell assets he does not own, hoping to buy back later at a lower price.

Beta   Coefficient relating the sensitivity of an investment's return to that of the whole market. Published betas usually refer to listed equity shares.

Bonus issue (or **scrip issue**)   Issue of additional shares pro rata to existing shareholders 'free' (i.e. in exchange for no cash or other assets).

Book value (BV)   Balance sheet amount shown for an asset. Under historical cost accounting usually means not 'value' but 'cost less any amounts written off'.

Budget   Financial or quantitative statement, prepared and agreed prior to the budget period by those responsible, reflecting the policies to be pursued during that period to attain agreed objectives.

Bull   Speculator expecting prices to rise, who may buy assets (or options to acquire them) hoping to sell them later at a profit (rather than 'use' them).

Business risk   The volatility of a business's operating profits, due to the specific assets owned, regardless of how they are financed.

Capital   (a) Paid-up ordinary shares; (b) capital employed; (c) contrasted with 'revenue'.

Capital allowance (or **writing-down allowance**)   Tax equivalent of depreciation of (some) fixed assets, calculated according to Inland Revenue rules. For most equipment, 25 per cent on declining balance.

Capital asset pricing model (CAPM)   Theory about how assets (especially securities) are valued. Key feature is distinction between two different kinds of risk: unique (or specific) risk which can be diversified away by shareholders owning a portfolio of shares, and non-diversifiable market risk.

Capital budgeting   Planning use of investment funds, usually including methods of evaluating capital investment projects.

Capital employed   Shareholders' funds plus long-term liabilities (= net assets, = total assets less current liabilities.)

Capital expenditure   Expenditure treated as an asset on the balance sheet, in contrast to 'revenue' expenditure which is written off as an expense in the profit and loss account.

Capital gain   Part of the 'return' to shareholder from investment in securities, stemming from increase in market value, not from dividends or interest.

Capital gains tax (CGT)   Tax at marginal income tax rate on personal real gains exceeding £5,800 per year.

Capital markets   Financial markets which deal in long-term finance, both debt and equity.

Capital rationing   Limit on the amount of capital available in a period, either internally or externally imposed.

Capitalize   Record expenditure as an asset, rather than write it off as an expense.

Cash discount   Reduction in amount payable for goods sold on credit, offered in exchange for prompt settlement.

Cash flow   Usually defined as 'retained profits plus depreciation' for a period.

Collateral   Asset serving as security for a loan.

Compounding to horizon (CH)   DCF method telling the interest rate which will compound the initial investment, by the horizon date, to the same amount as the project itself is expected to produce.

Conglomerate   Diversified group of companies whose subsidiaries operate in unrelated areas.

Consistency   Principle in accounting, and for other statistics, of treating similar items in the same way, to allow meaningful comparisons.

Consolidated accounts (or **group accounts**)   Accounts for a group of companies, 'consolidated' by combining the separate assets and liabilities of all subsidiaries with those of the holding (parent) company.

Constant purchasing power (CPP) accounting   Method of inflation accounting which adjusts historical money costs of various dates by means of the retail prices index. (Originally the 'C' was used to mean 'current'.)

Contribution   Sales revenue less variable costs, either in total or per unit.

Control   In management accounting, 'control' means: planning, comparing actual performance with budget, explaining significant variances, and acting to improve things.

Convertible loan   Loan convertible at holder's option into ordinary shares on prearranged terms.

Corporation tax (CT)   Tax payable by companies on taxable profits. 1994/95 rate 33 per cent > £1.5 million, or 25 per cent < £0.3 million.

Cost   Amount given up in exchange for goods or services received. In accounts it may appear either as an asset or as an expense.

Cost of capital   Usually = WACC, i.e. risk-adjusted weighted average of the (marginal) after-tax costs of equity and debt. The criterion rate of return for capital investment projects. May be either in money or in real terms.

Cost of goods sold (COGS)   Costs identifiable with stocks, for example: raw materials and bought-in components, direct labour and production overheads; but excluding selling, distribution and administrative expenses.

Coupon rate   Nominal rate of interest payable on fixed-interest securities.

Covenants   Conditions attached to loan agreements restricting borrower's freedom of action, for example *re* dividends, working capital, etc.

Creditors (or **accounts payable**)   Amounts due to suppliers for goods or services purchased on credit.

Criterion rate (or **hurdle rate**)   Required rate of return on investment project.

Currency debasement   Process of reducing purchasing power of currency as a deliberate act of policy; originally by fraudulently adding base metal to precious metal, in modern times by more sophisticated methods.

Current asset Cash or any asset, such as stocks or debtors, expected to be converted into cash (or consumed in the normal course of business) within twelve months from the balance sheet date.

Current cost accounting (CCA) System of current value accounting which continues to use money as the unit of account (unlike CPP), but shows assets and expenses at current replacement cost (normally) instead of historical cost.

Current liabilities (on **creditors:** amounts falling due within one year) Amounts owing to others (such as trade creditors or tax) payable within twelve months from the balance sheet date. May be split between short-term interest-bearing finance and the rest.

Current ratio Measure of liquidity, current assets divided by current liabilities. Rule of thumb: should normally be between 1½ and 2.

Current value May mean current replacement cost of asset, or net realizable value. Unlike historical cost, which is usually a definite known fact, current value can usually only be a hypothetical estimate.

Days' sales in debtors Debtors divided by daily sales (i.e. by annual sales revenue divided by 365). Ratio showing how much credit customers are taking. Needs adjusting for VAT

Debenture Long-term liability (Latin: 'they are owed').

Debt Negotiated interest-bearing borrowing (as opposed to 'equity'). May include short-term as well as long-term finance.

Debtors (or **accounts receivable**) Amounts due from customers for goods or services sold on credit. In the balance sheet, may include prepayments.

Debt ratio Balance sheet measure of financial gearing. In UK often: debt ÷ (debt + equity). In US often: debt ÷ equity.

Declining balance depreciation Depreciation method which charges each year a constant percentage of the declining net book value. Used by Inland Revenue for plant and equipment.

Deep discount bond Loan stock issued well below par (its redemption amount), so that much (or all) of the 'interest' yield comes by way of capital gain.

Deferred taxation Part of tax expense charged in accounts not payable for some time, due to timing differences between reported and taxable profits.

Depreciation Process of writing off the cost of a fixed asset, to spread the total net cost over its useful life and match against revenues.

Derivatives Financial instruments, such as options, 'derived' from underlying securities, such as ordinary shares. May relate to foreign currencies and to commodities, as well as to shares.

Dilution   Process which reduces a shareholder's equity interest when a company issues additional shares to other shareholders (for example, on conversion of debt or exercising of options).

Discount factor   Multiplier needed to reduce future cash flows to present value.

Discount rate   Interest rate used in making present value calculations.

Discounted cash flow (DCF)   Technique for evaluating capital projects, using interest rate as 'exchange rate over time'. Main methods: NPV, IRR.

Discounted payback   Payback period calculated using discounted (present value) amounts for cash inflows.

Disinvestment   Reducing investment by selling or abandoning asset(s).

Diversification   Adding or substituting investments with low or negative covariance with existing holdings, to help reduce total risk of portfolio.

Dividend   Cash payable to ordinary (or preference) shareholders, out of profits if declared by a company's directors. May be 'interim' or 'final'.

Dividend cover   Profits for a year divided by dividends.

Dividend payout ratio (DPR)   Reciprocal of dividend cover: dividends proposed for a year divided by profits available for the year.

Dividend yield (DY)   Dividends per share for a year (gross of income tax deducted), divided by the market price.

Double-entry accounting   System of recording business transactions based on their two aspects: a 'source' of funds and a 'use' of funds.

Earnings per share (EPS)   Profit after tax (and after minority interests and preference dividends) divided by the number of ordinary shares in issue.

Earnings yield (EY)   EPS divided by the market price per share.

Economic value added (EVA) (or **residual income**)   Profit for a period less interest (actual or notional) on total capital employed.

Equity   Ordinary share capital and reserves; (ordinary) shareholder's funds.

Equity beta   Coefficient relating the sensitivity of an equity share's return to that of the whole market. (Contrasted with **asset beta**.)

Exceptional items   Items disclosed separately in profit and loss account, unusual on account of size or infrequency of occurrence.

Expected value Weighted average of subjective probabilities applied to all possible anticipated outcomes.

Expenditure (or **cost**) Amount spent: may be either revenue (expense) or capital (asset).

Expense Amount written off against profit in respect of goods or services consumed, or other loss.

External finance Funds raised from 'outside' a company, such as borrowing or issuing new equity shares for cash. Contrasted with retained profits.

Extraordinary items Prior to FRS 3 defined as: 'profit and loss account items which appear "below the line" (used to calculate earnings per share), being (a) material, (b) not expected to recur frequently, and (c) derived from events or transactions outside the ordinary activities of the business'. FRS 3 now says almost everything that can happen is part of the 'ordinary' activities, hence extraordinary items are now extremely rare.

Factor Company which buys trade debts at a discount for cash.

Final dividend Second dividend for a year, after interim dividend.

Financial accounting External accounting, leading to published accounts for the shareholders and other 'outsiders'.

Financial lease Contract giving lessee use of an asset over most of its life, providing in effect another way to finance its 'acquisition'.

Financial objective (of a company) 'To maximize the wealth of the present ordinary shareholders.'

Financial risk Extra volatility of stream of equity earnings due to presence of debt in capital structure (financial gearing).

Financial year The 12-month period for which a firm prepares its accounts.

Finished goods Stocks of completed manufactured goods, held for sale.

First in, first out (FIFO) Method of valuing stock at cost, assuming most recent purchases remain in stock at the end of an accounting period.

Fixed asset Resource, either tangible or intangible, with long life, intended to be held for use in producing goods or services, not for sale in the ordinary course of business.

Flat yield Interest yield ignoring capital gain (or loss) on maturity. Annual interest divided by current market price.

Floating charge Charge which is not secured against specific assets, but which 'floats' over all (otherwise unsecured) assets, 'crystallizing' only on occurrence of specified events.

Fully diluted EPS What EPS would be if all outstanding conversion rights and other options were exercised.

Gearing   Proportion of debt in capital structure is 'financial gearing'. Proportion of fixed costs to total operating expenses is 'business gearing'.

Gilt-edged securities   UK government securities, regarded as 'risk-free' – *apart* from the risk of inflation.

Going concern   Assumption in accounting that a business entity will continue in operation for the foreseeable future.

Goodwill   Excess of purchase price paid to acquire another company over the 'fair value' of the net separable assets acquired.

Gross funds   Funds, such as pension funds, which are free of tax, hence able to recover income tax deducted at source from dividends.

Group accounts (or **consolidated accounts**)   Accounts for a group of companies, 'consolidated' by combining the separate assets and liabilities of all subsidiaries with those of the holding (parent) company.

Guarantee   Undertaking to be responsible for the debts of another (person or company) if the nominal debtor fails to pay in full.

Hire purchase (HP)   System of paying for an asset by instalments.

Historical cost (HC)   Traditional accounting convention of showing assets and expenses at actual past money cost (rather than, for example, at current value). CPP is an HC system, using constant purchasing power rather than money.

Holding company (or **parent company**)   Company owning more than 50 per cent of equity shares in subsidiaries, directly or indirectly; or controlling the composition of the board of directors.

Horizon   Point in future beyond which financial calculations are not made explicitly (though including a 'terminal value' makes them implicitly).

Horizontal merger   Combination of firms making the same kind of product.

Hurdle rate (or **criterion rate**)   Required rate of return on capital project.

Income bonds   Bonds on which interest is legally payable only if earned in the period, though unpaid interest is normally cumulated to be paid later when earnings permit.

Income tax   Tax payable on personal incomes, such as dividends or trading profits of partnerships or sole traders. For 1994/95, basic rate is 25 per cent, higher rate 40 per cent on taxable incomes above £23,700.

Incremental cash flows   Cash flows which occur as a result of action (such as investing in a capital project), but not otherwise. May include opportunity costs, such as foregone proceeds from selling an asset to be used in a project.

Index-linking (or **indexation**)   Linking a money amount to the rate of inflation as measured by the RPI. Examples: government securities, pensions, tax thresholds, capital gains.

Inflation   Rise in the general level of money prices, measured by the annual rate of increase in the retail prices index.

Inflation accounting   Constant purchasing power (CPP) accounting. (Current cost accounting (CCA) (q.v.) is *not* a method of adjusting accounts for general inflation.)

Inflation premium   Part of the nominal (money) rate of interest, depending on the expected future rate of inflation.

Insiders   Individuals held by law to have 'inside' knowledge of events not yet made public, and therefore prohibited from dealing in relevant shares on stock exchange, or from passing on inside information to others.

Insolvency   Inability to meet financial obligations.

Interest rate   Annual rate of compensation for borrowing or lending (money) comprising: (a) pure time-preference, (b) inflation premium, and (c) risk premium.

Interim dividend   First (of two or more) dividends payable in respect of a year's profits, the last being the final dividend.

Intermediaries   Financial institutions which separate borrowing from lending and may alter the time-maturity of loans. They profit from economies of scale and specialization, and reduce risk by diversification.

Internal finance   Raising funds from 'within' a company, usually referring to retained profits (plus depreciation), or perhaps disinvesting in assets.

Internal rate of return (IRR)   Rate of discount which, when applied to a capital project's expected cash flows, produces a net present value of zero.

Inventories (see **stocks**)

Investment (real)   Fixed capital formation, investment in fixed assets or stock.

Investment (financial)   Acquisition of a security, often from an existing holder via the secondary market. Hence 'financial' investment need not imply 'real' investment.

Investment trust   Company which holds a portfolio of securities.

Irredeemable   Loan stock with no maturity date, whose annual interest is a 'perpetuity'. May be redeemable at issuer's option (*not* at holder's).

Last in, first out (LIFO)   Method of valuing stock at cost, very rare in UK where it is not allowed for tax purposes. Assumes that most recent purchases have been used up in current period, leaving (much) earlier purchases in stock at end.

Lease   Commitment (by the 'lessee') to pay rent to the owner ('lessor') in return for the use of an asset. May be 'financial' (long-term) or 'operating' (short-term).

Liability   Amount owing to a creditor.

Limited company   Form of business organization in which the liability of the owners (shareholders) for the company's debts is limited to the fully paid nominal amount of their share capital. Abbreviated to 'ltd' (or to 'plc' (public limited company) for larger companies).

Liquidation (or **winding up**)   Legal process of ending a company's life, by selling all its assets for cash, paying off the creditors (if possible), and distributing any residual amount to the shareholders.

Liquid resources   Cash in hand and at bank, plus short-term marketable securities.

Listed company   Company whose ordinary shares are listed on a stock exchange, as opposed to a private company.

Loan stock   Long-term loan (to a company or government agency), often tradeable on the stock exchange in the secondary market.

Long-term liability (or **creditors**: amounts falling due after more than one year)   Liability not due for settlement until more than twelve months after the balance sheet date.

Loss   Negative profit, where expenses exceed sales revenue. Though not the aim, often the result of business (especially after allowing for (a) inflation and (b) interest on equity capital).

Mainstream corporation tax   Main company liability to UK corporation tax on taxable profits, payable nine months after the end of the financial year; reduced to the extent of ACT, paid at the same time as dividends.

Management buy-out   Acquisition of a business by a team of its senior managers who themselves take an equity interest, but largely financed by venture capitalists, often mainly with debt.

Market risk   The non-diversifiable part of the total risk attaching to an investment, measured by 'beta'.

Matching principle   The accounting principle according to which balance sheets carry forward expenditures as assets only if there are expected to be sufficient sales revenues (or disposal proceeds) in future against which to match them.

Matching the maturity   Process of 'matching' the time period of assets and liabilities, to reduce risk.

Maturity   Time at which a loan falls due for repayment.

Merger   A combination of two or more formerly independent business entities into a single enterprise.

Minority interests (MI)   Equity interests of minority shareholders in subsidiary companies which are less than wholly owned.

Modern portfolio theory (MPT)   Distinguishes non-diversifiable 'market risk' from unique risk, which a properly diversified portfolio can eliminate.

Monetary asset/liability   Asset receivable or liability payable in terms of money, as opposed to 'real' assets such as stocks or tangible fixed assets.

'Monetary loss/gain'   In CPP accounting, the loss arising (in terms of constant purchasing power, *not* of money!) in times of inflation from holding cash or other monetary assets (or the gain from owing monetary liabilities). Not taxable.

Negative interest rate   'Real' interest rate, after-tax and net of inflation, which may be negative: (a) because, while the inflation premium is tax-deductible, the 'monetary gain' from inflation is not taxable; or (b) because the actual rate of inflation exceeds that anticipated in the inflation premium.

Net assets (or **capital employed**)   Total assets less current liabilities (other than short-term interest-bearing finance) = fixed assets + operating working capital.

Net book value (NBV)   Cost (or valuation) of assets, less amounts written off.

Net current assets (or **working capital**)   Current assets less current liabilities.

Net dividend   Amount of cash dividend payable to ordinary shareholders, less income tax deducted at source (ACT).

Net present value (NPV)   Discounted estimated future cash inflows minus (discounted) cash outflow(s). If positive, indicates prima facie acceptability on financial grounds of capital project (using discount rate as hurdle rate).

Net realizable value (NRV)   Net amount for which asset could currently be sold. If less than cost, used for valuing stocks.

Net terminal value (NTV)   As for NPV, but with cash flows compounded to future horizon date instead of discounted back to present (value).

Nominal value (or **par value**)   Face value of security, unrelated to current market value. Usually refers to ordinary shares, with nominal value often of 25p each or £1 each, or to government securities per £100 of stock.

Offer for sale   Method of selling ordinary shares to public.

Operating lease   Lease other than a financial lease, usually for a short period of time.

Opportunity cost   The hypothetical revenue or other benefit that might have been obtained by the 'next best' alternative course of action, which was forgone in favour of the course actually taken.

Option   Right to buy or sell a security or other asset at a pre-stated price, within a certain period of time. = 'derivative'. Or, more generally, simply the right (not the obligation) to take a particular course of action in future.

Ordinary share capital   Capital of a company, consisting of the amount called up on issued ordinary shares.

Owners' equity   Ordinary shareholders' funds.

Partnership   Form of enterprise with two or more partners (owners), each with unlimited personal liability to meet all the firm's debts in full.

Payback   Method of evaluating capital projects which measures how long before the initial investment is 'paid back' by later cash inflows. The method ignores cash inflows *after* payback, so does *not* measure profitability.

Perpetuity   Annuity payable for ever.

Placing   Method of issuing shares to clients of brokers.

Portfolio   Group of different investments held by a single owner, which diversifies away some of their 'unique' risk.

Post-project audit   The process of comparing part or all of a capital project's outcome after the event with the ex ante forecast.

Preference share capital   Form of share capital entitled to fixed rate of dividend (usually cumulative) if declared, and to repayment of a fixed sum on liquidation, with priority over ordinary shares ('equity').

Prepayment   Expense paid in advance of the period to which it relates, shown on the balance sheet as a current asset, often combined with debtors.

Present value (PV)   Discounted amount of future cash flows.

Price/earnings (P/E) ratio   Market price per ordinary share divided by the most recent annual earnings per share.

Primary market   Market for securities which raises new money from the public.

Privatization   Selling off government holdings in businesses.

Profit   Surplus of sales revenues over expenses usually for a period.

Profit and loss (P&L) account   Accounting statement showing the result (profit or loss) of business operations for a period, usually one year.

Profit before interest and tax (PBIT)   Operating profit before deducting costs of financing and tax.

Profit margin   Operating profit (before interest and tax) as a percentage of sales revenue. Profit margin × net asset turnover = return on net assets.

Profitability index (PI) DCF method which divides PV of inflows by PV of investment outflows (instead of, like NPV method, deducting PV of investment outflows from PV of inflows). Ratio > 1.0 signals 'go'.

Project finance Method of finance whose repayments (and perhaps interest) are tied to a project's operating results.

Prospectus Advertisement to public about an issue of securities.

Prudence (or **conservatism**) Convention of accountants to provide in full for all known losses in accounts, but to recognize sales revenue (and profit) only when 'reasonable certainty' exists. Sometimes clashes with matching principle.

Public limited company (plc) Modern name for large limited company.

Purchasing power (or **value of money**) What money will buy in 'real' terms, usually measured by the 'basket of goods and services' comprising the constituent items in the retail price index.

Purchasing power parity (PPP) theorem Theorem that (in the 'long run') the relative exchange rates of currencies will vary in proportion to the relative rates of currency debasement.

Raw materials Input to manufacturing process, held for a time as stocks.

Realization The concept in accounting that sales revenue (and therefore profit) is recognized only when it is 'realized' in cash, or in other assets the ultimate cash realization of which can be assessed with reasonable certainty.

'Real' terms Amounts expressed after adjustments to allow for inflation.

Receiver Official managing a company's affairs, on behalf of debenture holders or others, often as a preliminary to liquidation.

Redemption Repayment of loan or preference share capital.

Redemption yield Yield on loan stock including element of capital gain (or loss) anticipated when the principal is repaid at par on maturity, in addition to the 'flat' yield of annual interest.

Reinvestment rate Assumption (explicit or implicit) about the rate of return a firm can earn on cash inflows 'reinvested' during a capital project's life.

Replacement cost Amount for which it is currently estimated that an asset held could be replaced.

Required rate of return (or **hurdle rate, criterion rate**) The rate of return needed for a capital project to be profitable, used as the discount rate for NPV.

Reserves Shareholders' funds other than paid-up share capital, including: share premium, revaluation reserves, cumulative retained profits. These represent past sources of funds; they may not be currently available in cash.

Residual income (RI) (or **economic value added**)   Profit less a capital charge representing interest on total capital. May be before or after tax.

Residual value   Net realizable value of fixed asset at the end of its useful life.

Retail prices index (RPI)   Monthly government statistic measuring the weighted average of money prices of a representative 'basket of goods'. Based on January 1987 = 100.

Retained profits (or **retained earnings**)   Amount of profits earned by a company not paid out in dividends (either for current period or cumulatively).

Return on capital employed (ROCE) (see **return on net assets**)

Return on equity   Profit after tax divided by shareholders' funds.

Return on funds employed (ROFE) (see **return on net assets**)

Return on investment (ROI) (see **return on net assets**)

Return on net assets (RONA) (or **ROCE, ROFE, or ROI**)   Operating profit before interest and tax, divided by net assets (= by total assets less current liabilities other than short-term interest-bearing finance).

Revaluation   Process of including asset in accounts at estimated current value when higher than historical cost.

Revaluation reserve   Increase in shareholders' funds needed to 'balance' the increase in net book value of assets due to revaluation.

Revenue   (a) Sales revenue; or (b) as contrasted with capital, relating to the profit and loss account rather than to the balance sheet.

Rights issue   Issue, usually of ordinary shares, to existing shareholders, to raise cash.

Risk   Volatility about a mean (average) 'expected value'. More loosely, possibility of loss (either likelihood or extent). Sometimes treated as synonymous with uncertainty.

Risk premium   Part of interest rate relating to perceived risk of investment. The risk premium on the whole market is estimated at 8.0 per cent a year.

Risk-free rate of return (R_f)   Rate of return available on government securities. An inflation premium may be included.

Sales revenue (or **turnover**)   A firm's gross trading income for a period.

Scrip issue (see **bonus issue**)

Secondary market   Market for securities in which existing holders can sell, and buy, without involving the original issuer.

Secured loan Liability 'secured' on an asset, with lender having legal right to the proceeds from the sale of that asset on liquidation, up to the amount of the liability.

Security (or collateral) Legal charge on asset(s) by lender. In the event of default, the lender is entitled to priority of repayment out of the proceeds of disposal of the charged asset(s).

Security (share) Any stocks or shares, usually listed.

Selling short Selling assets not owned, in the hope of buying back later after the market price has fallen.

Sensitivity analysis Method of seeing how much difference it makes to alter key variables. Allowing for interdependence is tricky.

Share Partial ownership of ordinary (or preference) capital of company.

Shareholders Usually refers to ordinary shareholders, who own company in proportion to number of shares held (but may also mean preference shareholders).

Shareholders' funds (or capital and reserves) Amount shown in company (and group) balance sheets as attributable to ordinary shareholders.

Share premium Excess of issue price over nominal value of shares.

Share split Process of dividing share capital into more shares of smaller nominal amount each. Reduces market price per share pro rata, without affecting the total market value.

Short-termism Alleged failure to take a 'sufficiently' long-term view.

Solvency Ability to settle liabilities when due.

Specific risk (or unique risk; diversifiable risk) Part of total risk, which can be diversified away by holding a suitable portfolio.

Speculator Anyone who acts on view about the uncertain future.

Spin-off Distribution by a parent company to its shareholders of shares in a subsidiary.

Stag Bull of new issues.

Stewardship Original basis for financial accounting, to account regularly to dispersed shareholders. Partly intended for protection of steward.

Stocks (or inventories) Holdings of goods, either as raw materials or components, work-in-progress, or finished goods, with a view to sale (perhaps after further processing) in the ordinary course of business.

Stock turnover Annual cost of goods sold divided by value of stocks held.

Straight-line depreciation Method of writing off net cost of fixed asset in equal instalments over its estimated useful life.

Subsidiary Company most or all of whose equity shares are owned by another (its 'holding' or 'parent' company).

Synergy What is hoped on merger to make $2 + 2 = 5$. Often elusive.

Taxable profit Differs from 'profit before tax' in accounts: (a) by deducting writing-down allowances instead of (book) depreciation; (b) by any accounting expenses disallowed by tax authorities; and (c) by any timing differences.

Taxation In company accounts means UK corporation tax plus any foreign tax on profits earned abroad. Excludes other taxes.

Tender method Method of issuing shares to the public, leaving the price to be settled by demand for the shares.

Term loan Loan, probably from a bank, for a fixed period of time, often between one and five years.

Term structure of interest rates The pattern of interest rates over different periods of time, for example, from three months to twenty-five years.

Terminal values Amounts (expected to be) recoverable at the 'end' of a capital project's life.

Time preference Ratio between someone's valuation of a good now and the same person's valuation of an otherwise identical good at some future date.

Trade credit Normal business arrangement to buy and sell goods 'on credit', that is, not settling in cash until some time later.

Transaction cost The cost of undertaking a transaction, for example, taxes, commissions, administrative costs, and so on.

True and fair view, a Aim of financial accounts, implying the use of generally accepted accounting concepts and conventions.

Turnover (see **sales revenue**)

Uncertainty Lack of knowledge about the future. Differs from 'risk', which usually assumes known probabilities of all possible outcomes.

Underwriter Person or firm agreeing, for a fee, to meet the financial consequences of a risk, for example on new share issues.

Ungeared beta (see **asset beta**)

Unique risk (see **specific risk; diversifiable risk**)

Unit of account The numeraire in accounting. Normally the monetary unit (as in HC and CCA); but in times of inflation CPP accounting suggests an alternative – the constant purchasing power unit.

Unit trust Financial enterprise holding a range of securities; suitable vehicle for a small unit-holder to spread his risk.

Unlisted company Company whose shares are not quoted (listed) on the stock exchange. Hence shareholders may find it hard to sell their shares.

Unlisted securities market (USM) Market for securities of companies too small or new for full listing; subject to less stringent rules.

Unrecovered ACT ACT unable to be fully set off against mainstream corporation tax, for example due to losses or to profits earned abroad.

Vertical format Modern form of accounts, showing net assets and capital employed underneath each other in balance sheet; and deducting expenses seriatim from sales revenue in profit and loss account.

Vertical merger Combination of two (or more) businesses engaged in different stages of production process in same industry; for example, a brewery buying pubs, or a tyre manufacturer buying a rubber plantation.

Wealth Well-offness, expressed in terms of money, normally related to ultimately marketable assets.

Weighted average cost of capital (WACC) Average of the after-tax (marginal) costs of various kinds of finance (debt, equity, etc.), 'weighted' by their market value (or by their book value).

Winding-up (see **liquidation**)

Working capital (or **net current assets**) Excess of current assets over current liabilities. May be negative.

Work-in-progress (WIP) Partly completed stocks in a manufacturing business, valued at the lower of cost or net realizable value.

Write off To charge as an expense in the profit and loss account (or, rarely, against reserves).

Writing-down allowance (wda) (or **capital allowance**) Tax equivalent of (book) depreciation of fixed assets, calculated according to Inland Revenue rules.

Yield Rate of return on investment (usually security). Interest or dividend for a year, divided by the current market price.

Yield to redemption (see **redemption yield**)

Bibliography

Buckley, A., *Multinational Finance*, 2nd edn, Prentice Hall, 1992.

Buckley, A., *International Capital Budgeting*, Prentice Hall, 1995 (forthcoming).

Chew, D. H. Jr., *The New Corporate Finance: Where theory meets practice*, McGraw-Hill, 1993.

Clarke, R. G., Wilson, B., Daines, R. H. and Nadauld, S. D., *Strategic Financial Management*, Irwin, 1988.

Copeland, T., Koller, T. and Murrin, J., *Valuation: Measuring and managing the value of companies*, John Wiley, 1990.

Reid, W. and Myddelton, D. R., *The Meaning of Company Accounts*, 5th edn, Gower, 1992.

Stern, J. M. and Chew, D. H. Jr., *The Revolution in Corporate Finance*, Blackwell, 1986.

Ward, K. R., *Corporate Financial Strategy*, Butterworth-Heinemann, 1993.

Index